T0209780

PROGRESSIVE STEPS
to
SALVATION

PROGRESSIVE STEPS
to
SALVATION

Pastor Leon Brown

PROGRESSIVE STEPS TO SALVATION

iUniverse books may be ordered through booksellers or by contacting:

iUniverse
1663 Liberty Drive
Bloomington, IN 47403
www.iuniverse.com
1-800-Authors (1-800-288-4677)

ISBN: 978-1-6632-0261-1 (sc)
ISBN: 978-1-6632-0262-8 (e)

Library of Congress Control Number: 2020910239

Print information available on the last page.

iUniverse rev. date: 06/19/2020

God saved us from these great dangers of death,
and he will continue to save us. We have put
our hope in him, and he will save us again!
—2 Corinthians 1:10

Do not be shaped by this world; instead be
changed within by a new way of thinking.
Then you will be able to decide what God
wants for you; you will know what is good
and pleasing to him and what is perfect.
—Romans 12:2

That they all may be one; even as
thou, Father, art in me, and I in thee,
that they also may be one in us.
—John 17:21

Introduction

Until God opens the next door,
praise Him in the Hallway!
—Kelly Wahlquist

You'll never see the great things ahead of you, if
you keep looking at the bad things behind you.
—Author unknown

Solomon said, "Wisdom is the principle thing, get wisdom and in all of thy getting, get an understanding!" (Proverbs 4:7). The apostle Paul said, "Study to show thyself approved unto God, a workman that, that needeth not be ashamed, rightly dividing the word of truth" (2 Timothy 2:15).

Pastor Leon's Background

I currently live in Anchorage, Alaska. My military service (USAF) spanned thirty years and six months; I furthered my education along the way. I was given military assignments overseas in the Netherlands, Italy, Germany,

Turkey, and Thailand. My last duty was at Elmendorf AFB, Anchorage, Alaska, where I retired in 1991. Additional ministry travels have taken me to South Africa, Uganda, Estonia (the islands of Saaremaa, Rakvere, Tartu, and Kuressaare), the Dominican Republic, Panama, and New Zealand.

I earned an associate degree from the State University New York (SUNY), Albany; a bachelor's degree in counseling at the University of Tampa, Florida; a master's degree in counseling at Ball State University, Muncie, Indiana; and a PhD in counseling and ministry of philosophy from Trinity Theological Seminary, Newburgh, Indiana. I received apostolic training at the Apostolic School of Ministry in Pietermaritzburg, South Africa. In 1998, I founded the Agape Worship Center, Anchorage, Alaska. My ministry includes visits to several villages throughout Alaska. I have been broadcasting worship services on radio and television to the city of Anchorage for over twenty years.

My mother and father were Pentecostal preachers of the gospel. Traveling domestically and abroad gave me the opportunity to visit a great many ministries. With this experience, I have engaged other religious leaders concerning the gospel of Jesus Christ and His kingdom.

The Lord gave me a deeper understanding and a unique desire for further study and fasting to establish a stronger relationship so that I may see the unfolding of His Word. God gave me revelations with numerous insights into the preaching and teaching of the Word of

God. One major insight God gave me concerns salvation with a threefold aspect: spirit, soul, and body.

Progressive Steps to Salvation is about humanity's need for a greater understanding of complete salvation. I wish to reveal to God's people the definition of complete salvation! To be given complete or full salvation is to obey God's creation order and to experience redemption of the spirit, the soul, and the body. My prime focus is to bring believers to a full understanding of their threefold salvation according to the Holy Scriptures. I will progressively explain the scriptures. In 1 Thessalonians 5:23, we read that for the time of Christ's appearing, God's mandate is to have His sons and daughters be blameless in spirit, soul, and body!

The body of Christ needs a clearer understanding and a commitment to know the internal work of Christ on the spiritual journey. Many believers have been attacked by the enemy because of their spiritual blindness (soulish—emotions). They do not understand the internal work of Christ that they might otherwise use to set themselves free from all forms of demonic bondage. By revelation, David was able to sing this song: "Bless the Lord, O, my soul!" (Psalm 103:1) - [KJV]. Only after David was set free was he able to spiritually bless the Lord. The purpose of the internal work of Christ is to target the spirit, soul, and body and set humankind free! You shall know the truth—Jesus Christ—and He will set you free from the lie and deceptions of the enemy. However, I believe the specific needs (hurts and emotions) of the soul and the body are before us. Only the Bread of Life [Jesus Christ] is the sole satisfaction!

As it was in the garden of Eden, Eve and Adam lost their spiritual sight and fell into dark and evil soulish sight. Because of this downfall, the body of Christ needs divine help. The Father is able to reverse this problem by the application of His Word. The internal work of Christ is threefold, and in this season we must minister to the soul and body of a human being on the way to divine maturity.

Remember, it is the Father's work and creation order to bring full salvation to all believers. These are progressive steps that are set for growth, which is the desire of our Father. The Apostle Paul expresses the need for the human spirit, soul, and body of one who is in Christ to reach a position of blamelessness (1 Thessalonians 2:10, 5:23).

Our Father's creation order and work are both clearly progressive because His way comes to us in three steps. Several scriptures serve as examples: "A threefold cord is not easily broken" (Ecclesiastes 4:12); "Faith, hope and charity, these three" (1 Corinthians 13:13); "I am the way, the truth, and the life" (John 14:6); and "That ye may prove what is the good, and acceptable and perfect will of God" (Romans 12:2).

Christ is a threefold God. He is the Good Shepherd (John 10:1), the Great Shepherd (Hebrews 13:20), and the Chief Shepherd (1 Peter 5:4). In the Old Testament and New Testament, God revealed something to Moses concerning the initial three places in the tabernacle: the outer court, the holy place, and the holy of holies.

We must achieve that lofty position of being blameless before Christ. Total salvation of the believer is a mandate that helps the son or daughter of God to endure the difficulties that confront him or her as a good soldier. This salvation comes to us in three phases:

1. Being born again. This takes place in a moment in time (John 3:1–3). Nicodemus came to Jesus by night to receive Him in his heart. You must be born again.

2. Experiencing deliverance of the soul. Only the Word of God can transform a human being's soul. This phase has to do with derailed feelings, hurt emotions, and religious mind-sets arising from past experiences. Because of these things, the soul of humankind needs deliverance so as to be set free by Christ (Romans 7:23–24). Paul's initial salvation occurred on the road to Damascus, and his subsequent experience is found in the book of Romans. His third experience, progressive salvation, is discussed in Galatians 2:20.

3. The body of the believer experiencing and coming into compliance with the "crucifixion of the flesh" (Galatians 2:20). We read in Romans 7:14, "We know that the law is spiritual, but I am of the flesh, sold [into slavery] under sin." In this we see that the flesh was called to die Paul said, "It is no longer I who lives but Christ lives in me!"

Finally, many avid churchgoers have little knowledge of Christ's internal work of progressively bringing the believer to salvation through growth and spiritual maturity. This is the kingdom of God, being one with Christ and one in the spirit with a restoration of the soul and with spiritual death of the flesh. And the Lord set a mark [divine favor] upon Cain. He went and lived in Nod, east of Eden. [Gen 4:15-17].

Chapter 1

Now that I Am Saved!

It was the attack in the garden. It was the first Adam who lost everything, but the second Adam was set to retain and return to the Father's plan. God the Father's global plan for humanity includes you. When you were born as a human being, you became the object of extreme hatred and jealousy for Satan, a former archangel, and his hosts, for it is upon human beings, not angels, that God elects to display His grace, love, and mercy so as to bring believers to complete deliverance.

When Satan saw what God was doing in placing this puny creature in charge of his former domain, he immediately began to design a plan to plant rebellion within human beings and depose them from the position of lordship that God had given them when His grace was extended to the man and woman in the garden of Eden through the provision of substitutionary blood. The promise was made that someday God would send the Savior to be the Lamb of God.

1

After being outmaneuvered by God and failing with Adam and Eve, Satan took note that God had said the Savior would come through the seed of the woman. Satan continued to invade the affairs of humankind. He had managed to infiltrate the human race with other angelic creatures. The entire race was tainted by the demonic strain except for Noah and his family. God struck the devil with another mighty blow when He had Noah prepare an ark. However, Satan continued to work ceaselessly to drag men and women from a place of blessings to a life of idolatry. When the coming of the promised Messiah was near, there was a mighty satanic upheaval. Satan never gives up, but in Christ we have the victory.

Now that you are *saved* (i.e., you have repented of your sins, accepted Jesus as Savior, and confessed this via your mouth and believed it in your heart [Romans 10:9]), what is the next spiritual step that awaits you? God's mandate is for the believer to continue on to know the Lord. Your soul and body are subjected to further change with progressive development. According to 1 Thessalonians 5:23, 2:10, your spirit, soul, and body (flesh) must be blameless (faultless) at His Second Coming. The Father expresses and speaks to you threefold, meaning the Word of God will both purify your soul and crucify your body. Each part of the Christian life should bear evidence that one is set apart as holy to God.

God is calling each believer to[Pastors, elders, leaders] become one in Him as Christ and the Father are *one*! All of us who are spiritually mature should have this attitude. If you have a different attitude, God will make this clear to you. Therefore, in accordance with the scripture Philippians 3:14, I press toward the goal for the prize of the upward call of God in Christ Jesus. As you run, the Holy Spirit will cause you to search the scriptures to determine your path. We are commanded in John 5:39, "Search the Scriptures; for in them ye think ye have eternal life." "Therefore, put away all filthiness and rampant wickedness and receive with meekness the implanted word, which is able to save your souls. But be doers of the word, and not hearers only, deceiving yourselves" (James 1:21–22 ESV). In other words, don't be as a listener; instead, put the Word into practice.

Terminology

In taking up this new calling, having an understanding of the meanings of a believer's spirit, soul, and body is important. Throughout *Progressive Steps to Salvation* I will repeat these terms not merely because it will help you remember them but also because it will give you a deeper understanding of their meanings.

Body (Desires of the Flesh)

This is the natural human structure made of flesh. To live for the body is to have an existence and experiences without the things of the Spirit of God.

Spirit

We are each a spirit that has a body and a soul. The spirit and soul reside in the body, which is a temporary house. So our spirits, the Spirit of God, and our souls all will be with us in heaven. The order of importance is spirit first, soul second, and body last.

Soul

The soul is made up of the personality, the intellect, and the mind as it deals with the intellect, the will, the emotions, and the heart. This area of emotion includes traumas, hurts, and rejections. These things loom large in the soul/heart of a human being.

Will

With the will resides the power of choice. By exercising the will, one engages in deliberate action or intention.

Emotion

An emotion is a physical or mental response to what is happening. It may be a change in feeling, a behavior, or internal excitement with both superficial (i.e., of the mind) and deep (extremely strong) phenomena being elicited.

Mind

This is the thinking and perceiving part of consciousness, intellect, and reason.

Trauma

Trauma is a severe, sudden shock that has a permanent effect upon the personality. Many souls have been deeply hurt, thus changing their outlooks and behaviors. In the past at some of the churches I attended, many females expressed having been devastated. Their stories and their behaviors need added attention.

Designated Journey

In our progressive journey assigned by our Father, we will learn that the heart (soul) needs renovation and that the body must die in a spiritual sense. Why? We are living in a fallen world with a fallen nature that we acquired from the first Adamic nature (which easily gives in to temptations). Our ultimate goal is to run this race and seek to receive the last Adam, the "life-giving Spirit" (1 Corinthians 15:45 ESV). Our goal is to pursue Christ as the ultimate on our assigned journey.

As our journey (or race) continues, we will discover many inappropriate things about our lives that are not pleasing to our Father. The prophet Jeremiah speaks to the issues of the heart: "The heart is deceitful above all, and desperately wicked, who can know it? Jeremiah 17:9–10 we read, "Who can understand the human heart?

There is nothing else so deceitful; too sick to be healed" (NLT). ****Leon

In the *Deliverance Manual* by Gene B. Moody, the word for "soul" is *psyche*. This word defines the self—life, the emotions, the intellect, and the will. Paul shows us that a human being is a threefold being (1 Thessalonians 5:23). God's intention is to give the believer peace and holiness in his or her whole being: the spirit, the soul, and the body. The scripture teaches that prior to salvation a person is "dead in trespasses and sins" (Ephesians 2:1). Jesus comes in to the human spirit and brings it His life (1 John 5:11–12). Jesus has made adequate provisions for the whole person, but part of the responsibility now rests upon us as is shown in Philippians 2:13–15.

The word for "salvation" in this passage is *soteria*. Joseph H. Thayer's *Lexicon* gives as the primary meaning of this word "deliverance from the molestation of enemies." The picture becomes clear: Jesus has delivered our spirits from the power of Satan; now He says to us, "Work out your own deliverance from the molestations of enemies until you have freed both soul and body." To do this is to genuinely know Jesus.

A Daily Responsibility

Now that you are saved by the free gift of salvation, you must neither stop at this point of seeking Christ nor leave the pathway of your Christ-assigned journey to know the Lord. In other words, gaining knowledge of how to fight spiritual warfare must become a part of your daily life. It's an abomination to turn back to the world, "but (we are) among those who have faith and so are saved" (Hebrews 10:39 NIV). The Word of God is your weapon to continually resist the type of works you performed in the past. Second Corinthians 5:17 tells us that old things have passed away and we are now new creatures, but that doesn't stop Satan from bringing temptations to us. He sometimes tempts us with things we did or enjoyed in our past lives with the goal of defiling our souls and bodies. Remain prayerful, and be careful that the old sin nature does not become the "whipping post" and the middle ground between God and Satan. "Blessed is the man who endures trial, for when he has stood the test, he will receive the crown of life which God has promised to those who love him" (James 1:12).

Chapter 2

What Defiles a Person?

Spiritual warfare as part of Satan's continuous goal is meant to defile your life with a myriad of tools, thus causing you to become an abomination before Christ. Matthew 15:18 states, "But those things which proceed out of the mouth come forth from the heart; and they defile (become unclean, pollute or make common) the man." Matthew 15:19 says, "For out of the heart proceed *evil thoughts*, murders, adulteries, fornications, thefts, false witness, blasphemies" (emphasis added). And Matthew 15:20 says, "These are the things which defile a man." The believer's major point of attack is the thought life— the mind!

Examples of Defilement

Soulish Behavior [worldly activities]

There are two varieties of defilement we will discuss here that cause the type of worldly behavior that is an abomination before the eyes of the Lord. In my experiences as a pastor and senior leader, I have seen Satan doing some appalling and unlawful things in the church. Satan is drafting schemes to make a demonized team to marry the soul and body, thus defying the presence of the Lord. Rejection and stubbornness are both an abomination before the heart of our Lord Jesus Christ. The secret sins of the soul and body carry a serious and grave distinction that stands out before a holy God.

King Solomon alludes to the particular issue of sins of the soul and body as being one in Proverbs 6:16–19: "These six things (soulish and bodily behavior) doth the Lord hate; indeed, seven are repulsive to our Father: a proud look (attitude that makes one overestimate oneself and discount others), a lying tongue, hands that shed innocent blood, a heart that creates wicked plans, feet that run swiftly to evil, a false witness who breathes out lies (even half-truths) and one who spreads discord (rumors) among brothers" (NKJV). Furthermore, they had no restraints in the pulpit, therefore, there were evil and countless behaviors that dishonored the Holy Father.

Remember that the scriptures tell us, "The love of Christ restrains us" (2 Corinthians 5:14). It is my strong opinion that some among the body of Christ (God's people) are off course (i.e., they lack knowledge or misunderstand). This is so because they have been subject to a lack of teaching or erroneous teachings. Whatever is in the leader's heart is being disseminated to the pew. God says, "Blessed are the pure in heart, for they shall see God by revelations." In order to preach the purest Word of God, we must be purposeful, relational, and honored by the Word of God. God's people are very important; it is necessary for the sons and daughters of God to receive and feed on the Word of God. As it is prayed, "Give us this day our daily bread" (Matthew 6:11). However, if our daily bread is counterfeit, then that which is counterfeit is passed to the congregation with the same impurities.

The Prodigal Son's Behavior

The prodigal son in Luke 15:11–22 was rebellious and wasteful. He was lost, forsaking family, but he eventually returned to the cry of his father. Similarly, if the pastor's heart and the motives are not pure, then the congregation will feed on erroneous teachings. The intent of this message is to demonstrate the fact that the mind of the soul and the mind of the body must be transformed and restored to full compliance according to the Word of God. Equally important, the people of God must be mindful and be doers of the Word by taking the responsibility to study the Word and search the scriptures and put what they say into practice. The Bereas of Macedonia would search the scriptures daily to see whether the teaching they'd just heard was true (Acts 17:10). According to God's Word,

"These were fairer minded than those in Thessalonica in that they received the Word with all readiness and searched the Scriptures daily to find out whether these things were so" (Acts 17:11).

David's words welcome a greater presence of Christ: "Seven times a day do I praise thee because of thy righteous judgments" (Psalm 119:164). Our Father is blessing us right now because He has done great things and continues to do great things. "Our soul is escaped as a bird out of the snare of the fowlers: the snare is broken, and we are escaped" (Psalm 124:7 NASB). Once our souls escape the snares, then they will be repositioned in the divine order. That divine order is in maximum submission to the human spirit. In order to live above the bad behavior, we must obey the Word and the power of God, which enables us to live victorious lives. It's God's mandate that we seek the Lord and obey the Word of God, "for as many as are led by the spirit of God, they are the sons of God." [Rom.8:14]

Chapter 3

Promises of Redemption

These perilous times are unwelcoming and frightening, but if there is to be any hope, it is in Christ. The prophet Isaiah said, "Arise, shine; for thy light is come, and the glory of the Lord has risen upon thee. For, behold, the darkness shall cover the earth, and gross darkness the people, . ." (Isaiah 60:1–2).

Even with these severely deep-seated issues in the lives of many, Almighty God is well able to save the multitudes. Regardless of how dark the situations that surround us seem to be, God's promises remain before us as promises of hope.

Awake, awake to righteousness; in other words, God wants a relationship with you. The Father has countless ways of bringing redemption to His people even as they cry out to Him. Regardless of your spiritual status, the Father is there as you cry out to Him. Did He not say, "And, lo, I am with you always, even unto the end of the world. Amen" (Matthew 28:20)? Regardless of your status, God "will never leave you nor forsake you." This is the definition of the agape love that the Father has bestowed upon His sons and daughters. Father, open the eyes of Your sons and daughters so that they may see and understand this unconditional love that abounds to all humanity.

Family: Unconditional Love

There were troublesome days in Abraham's tent. Remember the dark days of Hagar and Ishmael her son, both of whom were sent out into the desert? The heart of the Father heard their son's cry, and He met their needs in spite of their spiritual status because God's love supersedes all conditions of humankind. This is the Father's love manifested when desperation in prayer prevails. When the soul of a person cries out for deliverance, God is well able to rescue that hurting soul. Agape love (regardless of the sin, unconditional love is given preeminence) operates on the basis and according to the character of an unconditional loving Father. This love is very important to His people and not their character or behaviors. In Genesis 16:13, about Hagar's crisis, God expresses His loving-kindness for all His people regardless of their status. He cares and constantly manifests His love. Hagar called on the name of the Lord, who spoke to her. "You are a God of seeing," she said. "Truly here I have seen Him who looks after me." The ultimate expression is that God cares for His people and always leaves hope because He is the Father of unconditional love.

It is clearly expressed here that the Father of mercy loves and cares for all people regardless of their situations. God is a God of agape love and great redemption in spite of our varied destitutions. God is the greatest Redeemer, and He cares and demonstrates His love far beyond our ability to understand. "Blessed by the God and Father of our Lord Jesus Christ, the Father of mercies and God of all comfort" (2 Corinthians 1:3 NET). "In him we have redemption through his blood, the forgiveness of our trespasses, according to the riches of his grace" (Ephesians 1:7 NASB). He is the supreme lover and deliverer of all humankind.

God's Unfailing Love

According to 2 Samuel 14:14, "We must all die; we are like water spilled on the ground, which cannot be gathered up again. But God will not take away life, and he devises means so that the banished one will not remain an outcast."

Jesus Christ has come to bring deliverance to every believer's soul and body because of His unfailing (unconditional) love and promise for His people. Here the Father clearly states His heart, filled with love for us: "If my people who are called by my name humble themselves, and pray, and seek my face and turn from their wicked ways, then I will hear from heaven and will forgive their sin and heal their land" (2 Chronicles 7:14). It is the heart of the Father to continue to express forgiveness because

He desires to have a family of sons and daughters growing up and developing into His image and likeness.

Quest for Victory

Two issues of the unredeemed soul (heart) are perpetual spiritual warfare and a mandate for victory. It is a constant effort one must make if one wishes to overcome darkness in the heart. David is our example: "O God create in me a pure heart and renew a right spirit within me" (Psalm 51:10). The heart (soul) must relate to the spirit, and the human spirit relates to the Holy Spirit. As these two become one, the washing and cleansing of the soul takes place. Again, the Holy Spirit relates only to a human being's human spirit! In the process of becoming one, the soul and flesh can be renewed.

Paul said, "When I would do good, evil is present." The Bible teaches us that as human beings, we are engaged in a continuous battle—spiritual warfare—between the Adamic soul and Christ's Spirit. Romans 8:7 says, "Because the carnal mind (soul) is enmity (enemy, hatred, hostility, ill-will, defamation, envy, and malice) against God: for it is not subject to the law of God, neither indeed can it be." You are born with a fallen nature, an Adamic mind, and this is the reason you have need of the rebirth of the spirit, renewal of the soul, and deliverance of the flesh.

You have an alternative source of behavior that flows either from the soul nature of your Adamic being or from your born-again nature. "God has poured into every believer's earthen vessel; but we have this treasure in earthen vessels that the excellence of the power may be of God and not of us" (2 Corinthians 4:7). Christ is the righteousness, peace, and joy in the Holy Spirit poured out to every believer. You have a choice; it's all between you and the Father. Your behavior will manifest itself either out of your spirit or out of your soul. Please read and meditate intently upon this principle. You have the key; you can choose either life or death (Deuteronomy. 30:19). You have been admonished to be a doer of the Word (James 1:21–22), washing your sins away. In Ephesians 5:26 we find reinforcement of God's promise: "That He might sanctify and cleanse her (as also with His church, the body of Christ) with the washing of water by the Word."

It is said:

> For, brethren, ye have been called unto liberty; only use not liberty for an occasion to the flesh, but by love serve one another. For all the law is fulfilled in one word, even in this; "Thou shalt love thy neighbor as thyself." But if ye bite and devour one another, take heed that ye be not consumed one of another. This I say then, walk in the Spirit, and ye shall not fulfil the lust of the flesh. For the flesh lusted against the Spirit, and the Spirit against the flesh: and these are contrary the one to the other: so that ye cannot do the things that ye would. But if ye be led of the Spirit, ye are not under the law. Now the works of the flesh are manifest, which are these; adultery, fornication, uncleanness, lasciviousness, idolatry,

> witchcraft, hatred, variance, emulations, wrath,
> strife, seditions, heresies, envying, murders,
> drunkenness, revellings, and such like: of which
> I tell you before, as I have also told you in time
> past, that *they which do such things shall not inherit
> the kingdom of God*. (Galatians 5:13–21; emphasis
> added)

According to the scriptures, "And the Lord said to Cain, why are you angry? And why do you look sad and dejected? If you do well, will you not be accepted? And if you do not well, sin crouches at your door; its desire is for you, and you must master it" (Genesis 4:6–7). Cain had let anger, rage, and jealousy take hold of him. Instead of repenting of his disobedience to God concerning sacrifices, he decided to destroy the object of his anger. He murdered his brother, hid his body, and pretended he didn't know anything about it. God was not deceived by this act; neither was the devil. For God looked into Cain's heart and saw all the evil there. Cain could have confessed his sin, but he did not. Instead he lied. "And now you are cursed by reason of the earth, which has opened its mouth to receive your brother's [shed] blood from your hand. When you till the ground, it shall no longer yield to you its strength; you shall be vagabond on the earth" (Genesis 4:11–12). Even at this point Cain could have repented and been forgiven, but he would not repent. In fact, he was telling God that God would have to accept him because of his fine gift.

There is nothing we can offer God that is fine enough to cause him to accept us. It is only by accepting Jesus

Christ as Savior and afterward living by God's directives that we may be acceptable to God. Cain began to tell God about the harshness of his sentence. In the light of his murder of his brother, this attitude shows his opposition to God's law.

Chapter 4

Righteousness: Feed the Spiritual Truths

Heed the Father's warning: "My people are destroyed for a lack of knowledge" (Hosea 4:6). About His law, which reveals His will, it is said, "In bringing his offering, Cain so did which was from the fruit of the ground, but God had no respect for Cain nor his offering" (Genesis 4:5).

"Cain brought his offering from the ground that was cursed" (Genesis 3:17). God cursed the ground because of the disobedient Adam, the first man. Cain's reaction was to express intense anger toward God. Righteousness is defined as maintaining a continuous stand of obedience toward the Father. And the Lord set a mark [divine favor] upon Cain. He went and lived in Nod, east of Eden. [Gen 4:15-17].

1. According to Malachi 2:6–8, "True instruction was in his mouth, and unrighteousness was not found on his lips. For the lips of a priest

should preserve knowledge, and men should seek instruction from his mouth; for he is the messenger of the Lord of Hosts. But as for you, you have turned aside from the way; you have caused many to stumble by the instruction; you have corrupted the covenant of Levi, says the Lord of the hosts."

2. Show diligence and pray to the Father, who will reveal this to you while fasting. "The Word of God must be taught as the Bread of Life for both the lambs and sheep, just as Peter was instructed by our Lord Jesus Christ" (John 21:15).

3. "Because you (the priestly nation) have rejected knowledge, I will also reject you from being My Priest. Since you have forgotten the law of your God, I will also forget your children" (Hosea 4:6).

A *lack of knowledge* among the body of Christ is a major issue. Thus, there are several problems that have in part caused defeat, hurt, and blindness. From the pulpit to the pew, God's people have experienced much blindness. This blindness is a problem in the body of Christ even today. With the lack of excellent teachings of God's Word, Satan has taken advantage of the body of Christ and has done much damage, starting from the pulpit and moving on to the pew.

Chapter 5

Call for Deliverance: Soul and Flesh

This is all about the Father's love for His people, and they are blessed far beyond measure. Even His people understand this great promise of God.

Let Us Follow on to Know God

The Father has countless ways for you to know Him and to discover His ways! In Hosea 6:2 we find the call for repentance: "Come and let us return (repent) to the Lord, for He has torn us, but He will heal us; He has wounded us, but He will bandage us. After two days He will revive us; on the third day He will raise us up that we may live before Him." This is the spirit of resurrection, for He will raise us up at His appointed time.

God Calls for Deliverance

God calls for deliverance (freedom from demonic strongholds) because God's people must be set free and healed. Righteousness, peace, and joy is what the Lord speaks of in Romans 14:17. "He restores my soul; He leads me in paths of righteousness for his name's sake" (Psalm 23:3). The contents of the soul and the flesh both need the ministry of deliverance. Matthew 15:18 speaks to those needs because the content of the soul defiles the person. Yet many leaders refuse to preach deliverance. This does not move Jesus; rather, it is rebellion against the Father. There are now many ancestral, generational, and familiar spirits diverting the pathway for God's people because leaders refuse to preach the full counsel of the Father. For example, Jonah knew God's directive but refused to obey the Father's instructions.

According to 1 Peter 4:11, "Whoever speaks, as one who utters oracles of God … whoever renders service … in order that in everything God may be glorified through Jesus Christ." Jesus's message is found in Luke 4:17–19: "The Spirit of the Lord is upon me, for he has anointed me to proclaim that captives will be released, that the blind will see, that the oppressed will be set free, and that the time of the Lord's favor has come." Many sincere believers want this deliverance, but their leaders will not teach deliverance because demons are the author of fear and torment. I witnessed an event when a woman attended service; suddenly a strange sound was continuously uttered. To me the demonic voice was in conflict with the Word. The pastor asked her to leave the service. This sort of thing happens when the leader fails to recognize the need to set believers free.

God's Word says, "And the seventy returned again, with joy, saying 'Lord even the devils are subject unto us through thy name'" (Luke 10:17). Not only did the Lord send the twelve but also He sent seventy others (Luke 10:1). What amazed these people who were sent the most was their authority over demons. Demons recognize those who are sent (Acts 19:15; Mark 16:17). It is said, "And these signs will accompany those who believe; in my name they will cast out demons." After the return of the seventy, the Lord said, "I beheld Satan fall as lightning from heaven" (Luke 10:18).

Again, leaders of ministry, the people of God need help now. And if you are willing to help them, God is willing to bless all His sons and daughters, the believers.

Chapter 6

Five Major Doctrines – Progressive Steps!

In the book of Romans, there are five major doctrines to help reinforce the fact that there are five different levels to salvation. Each of these doctrines will reveal to the believer the progressive steps that are necessary to arrive in the position appointed by Christ. The five doctrines are as follows:

- condemnation
- justification
- sanctification
- glorification
- consecration

The sin of the first Adam caused the whole world to fall into the spirit of condemnation. God reckons you as His new creation. Only after your journey from condemnation (applicable to those without Christ) to justification (applicable to those who have accepted Christ as Savior) can you begin the third phase of your journey and fully engage in this process of sanctification (a cleansing and renewal of heart). Then glorification occurs when Christ's presence is manifested inwardly and outwardly. Finally, you continue to seek Him as a living sacrifice. These five steps sum it up: It is the Father's good pleasure to give you the kingdom.

These five major doctrines will enable every believer to progress and move forward in his or her development to become one with the Father. This is the believer's promise stated by the apostle Paul: "Now the Lord is that Spirit: and where the Spirit of the Lord is, there is liberty. But we all, with open face beholding as in a glass the glory of the Lord, are changed into the same image from glory to glory, even as by the Spirit of the Lord" (2 Corinthians 3:17–18).

In this progression, the old person is put away and the new person in Christ comes forth. Remember, Paul says, "Old things are passed away; behold, all things have become new." The scripture I am referring to is 2 Corinthians 5:17: "Therefore, if anyone is in Christ—that is, grafted in, joined to Him by faith in Him as Savior—he is a new creature, reborn and renewed by the Holy Spirit; the old things, the previous moral and spiritual condition, have passed away. Behold, the new things have come because spiritual awakening brings a new life."

Progressive Sanctification

The moment a person receives Jesus Christ as his or her Savior, he or she is set apart with Christ's purpose. "For by one Spirit are we all baptized into one body, whether we be Jews or Gentiles, whether we be bond or free; and have been all made to drink into one Spirit" (1 Corinthians 12:13). God sees the believer thus in the second Adam, which is described in 1 Corinthians 15:45–57, where we are no longer the image of first Adam in God's sight. We have been set apart. This happens the moment we receive Christ as our personal Savior. We now have a personal Savior and a personal relationship with the Holy Spirit. The Holy Spirit is a person who comes and makes Himself personal to the believer.

By way of introduction to the doctrine of sanctification, you should know that there is a progressive sanctification. By that I mean daily, we are progressively set apart more and more by the Word of God and by the Holy Spirit through experience and tribulation. This is contingent upon our obedience to the Word of God and willingness to follow in His footsteps. We are separated from the way of the world, the way of the fallen nature, the flesh, we are set apart from the way of Satan and demons, and we are moved to God's way and the way of the Bible. We grow in grace and in the knowledge of our Lord Jesus Christ (2 Peter 3:18).

We have the promise of a graceful future with our Father. The day will come when we the believers will be set apart completely from this old world and this fallen nature and sin. This is God's promise; we call it the ultimate sanctification. So shall we be with Jesus forever, even in our glorified bodies (Romans 8:29–30). We are being set apart for our husband at the marriage feast of the Lamb, where we will be joined throughout eternity, dwelling in the new heaven, the new earth, and the New Jerusalem.

Glorification and Consecration

This doctrine of sanctification is taught in Romans 5:12–21 and 8:13. This is the explanation of sanctification through the work of the Holy Spirit. By engaging the Word of God, purification is made progressive in gradual proportions, upgrading both the soul and the body. When the believer grows and reaches the stage of glorification, the fourth step, we will see, is the work of God, who promises us a new body. Then, when we come to the doctrine of consecration, it is our turn. We will be called on to present our bodies as "a living sacrifice, holy, acceptable unto God", "which is your reasonable service." Romans 12:1, [KJV] This reasonable service is to continue in righteousness in honoring the God.

You are not delivered until your emotions, gratifications, relationships, and feelings are refined and gradually emanate to be like Jesus (Romans 7:23 NASB).

"And now why tarries' thou? arise, and be baptized, and wash away thy sins, calling on the name of the Lord" (Acts 22:16).

Chapter 7

Christ's Redemptive Acts: The Reconciliation Process

His New Creation: Old Things Are Passed Away; All Things Become New (2 Corinthians 5:17)

Both the soul and the flesh must change by the power of God's authority and the power of the Holy Spirit. Christ Jesus is targeting the third entity of the believer, namely, the flesh. The flesh must be transformed by the Father for proper realignment according to the Word of God. It is the Father's directive that the total entity be purified and changed. The Word of God is a special cleansing agent to bring about purification ("That he might sanctify and cleanse it with the washing of water by the word" [Ephesians 5:26]). God's anointed leaders must use the oracles of God (1 Peter 4:11) to touch the three entities (spirit, soul, and body) of the believer. These must be purified and untarnished by the preaching of the Word of the Spirit of God. According to 1 Thessalonians 5:23, the threefold entity of the believer must be blameless at Jesus's Second Coming.

Christ: The Example for His Sons and Daughters

The apostle Peter speaks to this concept of Christ as the example for all believers. These scriptures target the flesh of the believer, as found in 1 Peter 4:1–2: "Since Christ suffered physically, you too must strengthen yourself with the same way of thinking that He demonstrated; because whoever suffers physically is no longer involved with sin" (1 Peter 4:1).

Jesus dealt with the problem of dominion. The Bible says in Romans 6:14, "Sin shall not have dominion over you: for ye are not under the law, but under grace." The keyword is *dominion* (*kurios*[1]), which means one is lord and master, that is, "to have or exercise rule or authority over; to lord over." "For in him all things were created in heaven and on earth, visible and invisible, whether thrones or dominions or principalities or authorities—all things were created through him and for him" (Colossians 1:16). It is the Father's righteous authority to give this to His sons and daughters. The sons and daughters of God are the Father's representatives on earth. The believer starts to rule and dominate according to His will.

---

[1] James Strong, *Strong's Greek and Hebrew Dictionary of the Bible*, #G-2962, s.v. "kurios."

Example of His Armor

The armor of God is a symbol for the protection that warriors make use of in a time of engaging in spiritual warfare or physical battle, whatever the case may be. As we cry out, it is compulsory that we be spiritually dressed in armor. Jesus informs us believers to arm ourselves with the same mind. The word *arm* is another keyword—*hoplizo*[2]— which means "to furnish, prepare, equip with arms; take up arms; to furnish or be armed fully." This arming leads us to Ephesians 6:13: "Wherefore take unto you the whole armor of God, that ye may be able to withstand in the evil day, and having done all, to stand." The whole armor of God is a panoply, that is, a complete suit of armor, both for offensive and defensive purposes. *Putting on the whole armor of God enables the believer to stand in fully equipped gear (such as a Sherman tank), while the devil comes at him or her with a small handgun.* To stand means to be established, positioned, confirmed—in a spiritual place of divine authority. This is how Jesus stood in the presence of His Father. This is Paul's extended metaphor of full battle dress.

You are called and anointed to put on the whole armor of God, to be fully dressed according to the Word of God, knowing that the battle belongs to the Lord. In all this, we need to have a spiritual understanding of God's plan to get us battle-dressed. Even Solomon said, "In all of thy getting, get an understanding." We must continue to seek His presence to become "fully dressed in His armor"

---

[2] James Strong, *Strong's Greek Dictionary of the New Testament*, #G-369t/6, s.v. "hoplizo."

(according to the Word of God) and thereby gain the victories as we journey in Him.

Take on the Armor of God

Daily, take on the whole armor of God. This armor is symbolic, to help aid in understanding of spiritual warfare! Paul is showing the believer that he or she has to be fully dressed to conduct effective and victorious warfare against the works of darkness. Isaiah reinforces the fact that weapons are formed against believers; therefore, God has prepared and dressed for the events to come! Each piece of armor represents a soldier in battle dress.

The Father uses this passage to encourage believers that while the devil is seeking devastation, our God is saying, *I have given you the equipment to walk and live a victorious life.*

Elements of the armor of God include the following:

Picture of a Roman Soldier in battle dress!

THE WHOLE ARMOR OF GOD!
Eph. 6:10-11 [NLT]

1. **Earthen vessels.** The body of the believer is symbolically of an earthen vessel or clay jars containing these great treasures. This is clear that our great power is from God, not from ourselves. [2 Cor.4:7] NLT.

2. **Helmet of salvation.** This provides protection of the thought life in that it is the covering for the head. It protects against things such as evil dreams, evil thoughts, and various forms of demonic attack and makes possible deliverance, removal of selfishness, and cleansing of the soul.

3. **Shield of faith.** A warrior of steadfast faith must have a protective shield to fight spiritual warfare. The shield is synonymous with effective strategies of the Holy Spirit.

4. **Breastplate of righteousness.** The soldier's front torso must be covered. The breastplate indicates right standing in Christ and spiritual position by faith.

5. **Sword of the Spirit.** This weapon is for protection; it is an offensive weapon rightly divining the Word of Truth.

6. **Belt of truth.** A soldier of righteousness embraces the truths of God's Word. The belt speaks of divine protection; the wearer is covered by the promises of the Lord.

7. **Feet shod with the preparation of God.**

a. Mobility is the primary purpose of shoeing oneself; it indicates that one is walking about as God's representative.

b. One whose feet are shod is prepared for being sent out for the commission, going to accomplish the purposes of the Father.

As we go, our Father is a man of war (Ex. 15:3,14:14). In day-to-day living, the soldier of the Lord must continue to remain battle-dressed because his or her adversary is ever on the prowl.

Chapter 8

Christ's Redeeming Acts of Love

Christ's Promises for His Sons' and Daughters' Future

"Fear not, for I have redeemed three; I have called thee by thy name; Thou art mine" (Isaiah 43:1). According to my understanding of the Word, God has given precious and great promises for His sons and daughters. He has proven His love and care for His people. I am saying to you, be careful and prayerful. God has demonstrated His true love, that is, the cross, in which you are partakers, and we shall be like Him. The biblical teachings identify His promises:

1. **Controller of spirit and conscience**
   "For the love of Christ controls, us, because we are convinced that one has died for all; therefore, all have died" (2 Corinthians 5:14 ESV).

2. **Sacrificial lifestyle**

   "And he died for all that those who live might live no longer for themselves but for him who for their sake died and was raised" (2 Corinthians 5:15 ESV).

3. **First natural, then spiritual**

   Often, the Father teaches the believer in many different ways to bring about increased understanding. In 1 Corinthians 15:46–47 we read, "The spiritual did not come first, but the natural, and after that the spiritual. The first man was of the dust of the earth; the second man is of heaven." The goal of our progression is as follows: "And just as we have borne the image of the earthly man, so shall we bear the image of the heavenly man" (1 Corinthians 15:49 ESV). That man is Jesus Christ!

4. **Power of transformation (Romans 12:1–2)**

   "From now on, therefore, we regard no one from a human point of view; even though we once regarded Christ from a human point of view, we regard him thus no longer" (2 Corinthians 5:16 ESV). "Therefore, if anyone is in Christ, he is a new creation; the old has passed away, behold, the new has come" (2 Corinthians 5:17).

   ✓ The old life has passed away.
   ✓ All things have become new in Christ (the body of Christ).

- ✓ *Your salvation is a onetime experience* (i.e., you have a new position in Christ).

- ✓ Sanctification is a progressive occurrence. By God's Word, the purification process starts internally. For a doer of the Word, all forms of evil will continue to badger the person with evil temptations.

- ✓ Fleshly desires—evil feelings, evil thoughts— will continue. These are known as battles of the flesh or as craving of the heart and body. Matthew 15:18–19 addresses the contents of the heart in response to what Jeremiah 17:4 says: "The heart is deceitful, above all and desperate wicked; who can know it?"

- ✓ The believer experiences deliverance. In Romans 1:16 we read that the Word of God is the power of salvation (deliverance). God is a man of war, and He is fighting for the body of Christ. These promises are forever real; they have been made unconditionally to His sons and daughters. Victory is always obtained through Christ, the mighty one!

- ✓ The believer will have to fight spiritual warfare. "The Lord shall fight for you, and ye shall hold your peace" (Exodus 14:14). This is evident upon the point of receiving salvation because the works of the flesh will offer many alternates—unrelenting attacks. In spite of it all, we are yet winners, and we know no defeat.

Chapter 9

Ministry of Reconciliation

"All this is from God, who through Christ reconciled us to himself and gave us the ministry of reconciliation; that is, in Christ, God was reconciling the world to himself, not counting their trespasses against them, and entrusting to us the message of reconciliation" (2 Corinthians 5:18–19). This is good news for the sons and daughters of God that they may live far above any manner of distractions, thus enjoying His presence. This is my unction: "No more conflict but rather a great understanding and coming together!"

In the first part of the threefold nature of mankind, Jesus Christ now dwells. Therefore the believer no longer practices sin or disrespects his or her holy Father in any way as a sinner (condemned). Such a believer strongly desires to become a seasoned son or daughter in Christ Jesus. The believer knows that there is more in store for him or her, far beyond the initial gift of spiritual salvation. As we pay close attention to God's Word and understand these spiritual promises for believers, I pray that all believers' eyes will be opened because of God's great blessings and promises found in His Word. According to the scriptures, the Father says that the believers "must be blameless in spirit, soul, and body at [Christ's] appearing" (1 Thessalonians 5:23).

Chapter 10

Unfolding Truths about Salvation

Threefold Salvation

Full salvation, from onset to completion, is given to believers in three phases. The phases include the spirit, the soul, and the body. Your initial point of salvation is a gift from the Father. Continued salvation is found in two remaining phases, soul and body, which require further restoration and deliverance if full threefold salvation is to be 100 percent achieved. The fullness of divine life is achieved in the passing of time by the Word, which brings cleanness and purification. According to Ephesians 5:26, the dynamic impact of God's Word causes cleansing and removes all veils of darkness. This the greatness of our Father!

God's Targeting

The word for "soul" is *psyche*. This word defines the self-life—the emotions, the intellect (mind), and the will. Paul shows us that humankind is a threefold being: "Your spirit and soul and body be kept sound and blameless" (1 Thessalonians 5:23).

Soteria is the word for salvation in this passage. *Thayer's Lexicon* gives as the primary meaning of this word "deliverance from the molestation of enemies." The picture becomes clear. Jesus has delivered our *spirits* from the power of Satan; now He says to us, "Work out your own deliverance from the molestation of enemies until you have freed your *spirit*, *soul*, and *body*" (emphasis added). As repetition goes, I purposely repeat these concepts to reinforce understanding. A lack of knowledge and understanding can occur if one fails to follow on and come to know and apply the Word of God to his or her life. There is no time to put off practicing diligence.

Chapter 11

Truth Set Free

The Father says two things here about "truth" and "set free": "Search the Scriptures: for in them ye think ye have eternal life: and they are they which testify of me" (John 5:39) and "If the Son therefore shall make you free, ye shall be free indeed" (John 8:36).

However, many believers do not know these things; therefore, countless believers continue holding on to their past, blindly deceived and stealthily attacked by Satan with hurts, emotions, rejections, abandonments, divorces, and bitterness in their souls. This attitude has greatly affected the so-called believer's progressive steps toward reaching the higher place of the Father. This type of ignorance places a false burden on the believer, and the designated assignment is delayed or placed on the shelf. Therefore, the minister should seek the heart of God for the believer and encourage the believer to follow on to know the Lord. God has given His sons and daughters the keys to the kingdom; therefore, the Spirit of God will deliver them!

There is a great need in the body for spiritual understanding, education, and developing into an active doer of the Word, a "purifier" (James 1:22), to experience a divine intervention of full deliverance. Many who are part of the body of Christ have not been taught about the regeneration of the soul and deliverance of the body. For example, I cordially speak with various believers concerning their spiritual development; either they do not have knowledge of progressive salvation or, once they receive the gift of salvation, they believe they are free of all sin (100 percent complete salvation). Many believers don't study or meditate. This is why the prophet says, "My people are destroyed for lack of knowledge: because thou hast rejected knowledge, I will also reject thee, that thou shalt be no priest to me" (Hosea 4:6).

God says that the spirit, soul, and body must be blameless at His appearing (1 Thessalonians 5:23). *I purposely repeat many points like this because this is God's creation order.* Several other supporting scriptures reflect the believer's goal, for example: "That ye may be blameless and harmless, the sons of God, without rebuke, in the midst of a crooked and perverse nation, among whom ye shine as lights in the world; holding forth the word of life; that I may rejoice in the day of Christ, that I have not run in vain, neither labored in vain" (Philippians 2:15–16).

Chapter 12

Genuine Messengers

Christ's Message

We are blessed of the Lord to have numerous promises, and yet it is a greater blessing to understand and embrace these great promises of grace. In my travels, I have observed numerous unqualified ministers; however, in their minds, they've attempted to preach His Word. In many cases, these ministers could not read or pronounce the different words in the Bible. Some have practiced preaching on certain scriptures, and that is all that comes out of their mouths. Since Peter didn't have the power of God's Word, he failed his time of testing and he momentarily forsook Jesus in the garden. In John 13:38, Jesus answered Simon Peter, "Will you lay down your life for me? Truly, truly, I say to you, the cock will not crow, till you have denied me three times." Jesus then said, "Let not your hearts be troubled; believe in God, believe also in me" (John 14:1).

Since we are His sons and daughters and He is the Father, we can no longer follow our own pathway. Jesus Christ clearly states in John 14:6, "I am the way, the truth, and the life: no man cometh unto the Father, but by me."

"The words of a priest's lips should preserve knowledge of God, and people should go to him for instruction, for the priest is the messenger of the armies of the Lord of heaven" (Malachi 2:7). This is clearly the way of Christ in that we should seek Him daily for the relationship we are called to engage in. This relationship is something about which the apostle Paul spoke: "I die daily because as we receive more light of the Word, then darkness must flee." David endorsed this fact concerning the light of Christ and His Word: "The entrance of thy words giveth light; it giveth understanding unto the simple" (Psalm 119:130). In many cases, the unqualified minister is often aided by his or her assistants, other ministers, or deacons. Therefore, the congregants are mixed up and depressed and often leave the ministry. As we read in Romans 10:14, "And how shall they hear without a preacher!" Only the Father draws sincere people to ministry. And there is real genuine life given through Christ.

Chapter 13

Responsibility of Ministers

God's ministers have a higher level of responsibility (James 3:1) before God to tell the truth. God holds the minister to a higher standard of responsibility than He does the layperson who does not teach. The minister will have to answer to God for every word that he or she has uttered to teach God's people. Some ministers just selectively omit certain portions of the Bible to preach for many different reasons; some don't believe in healing, reconciliation, or even speaking in tongues. The dynamics of salvation are such that we are constantly learning and will never know all until God finishes His teaching in eternity. If we had to wait until we were perfect to preach, then there would be no ministers.

I pity the minister who chooses not to teach an unpopular concept from the Word of God, such as deliverance, which accounted for about 25 percent of the ministry of Jesus Christ. The pastor should teach the whole Bible, not just the parts he or she likes. If there is any part of the Bible about which a minister is ignorant, he or she will experience grief when he or she has to answer to God on the Great Day of Judgment, as well as in the here and now. The minister must be given over fully to the Lord, being God's representative on earth. The minister is not his or her own; the minister or teacher belongs to the Father. In the midst of lack, the Father of hope—that is, Jesus Christ—is there.

His Word: Purification

The book of Malachi speaks about leadership—be it priest, bishop, or pastor—and their unrighteousness; that is how I know that salvation of the soul and body is progressive. The Word of God is a purifier in which its light drives out any form of darkness, anything that opposes the Father. Furthermore, the prophet Malachi says to leaders, "And he shall sit as a refiner and purifier of silver (redemption) and he shall purify the Sons of Levites and purge them as gold and silver, that they may offer unto the Lord an offering in righteousness" (Malachi 3:3). Only the Father is well able to take the issue at hand and make it prosperous.

I see this as God's standards and qualifications for His sons and daughters to come into His presence and offer up acceptable spiritual worship. For such is the kingdom of God: "It is not food or drink; instead, it is righteousness, peace and joy in the Holy Ghost" (Romans 14:17). These are the characteristics and contents that heaven provides.

Paul says that the ministry of reconciliation has been given to God's sons and daughters as ambassadors to represent Him on the earth as kings and priests—not only given but also imbued with the authority of the given Word and anointed to minister in the spirit of reconciliation.

Ordained Leaders

To prematurely represent Christ or assume to represent Christ is to seriously undermine the Father and the Word of God. Preacher, pastor, teacher, you must realize the seriousness of your calling to feed the flock of God (Malachi 2:6–8). For the ordained minister it is critical to obey the Lord and pursue Christ, thus enabling you to give the best pastoral care to God's people with the pure bread of life. John says, "It is the Spirit who gives life; *the flesh profits nothing.* The words that I speak to you are spirit, and they are life" (John 6:63; emphasis added).

In Malachi 2:8, a clear command is issued to certain priests regarding their responsibilities: "But you priests have left God's pathway! Therefore, your instructions have caused many to stumble into sin. You have corrupted the covenant I made with the Levites," says the Lord of Heaven's armies. Jesus Christ is our Pattern Son; therefore, we must repent and seek that which He has laid before us. The Lord's Word is "a lamp to my feet and a light to my path" (Psalm 119:105). The caller and the anointed priest are to be led by the Holy Spirit to teach God's Word. I have witnessed many men and women who have stood in the pulpit and have not prepared themselves for that particular event. Therefore, much prayer is in order and very needed at that moment.

Hosea tells us that the people perish for a lack of knowledge. It with great emphasis that the Father expresses great concern for the purification of the threefold human being. The creation order of the Father is His mandate to set things into divine order, meaning the human spirit, soul, and body. God's Word must be given preeminence. These scriptures are very important to the body of Christ because the love of the Father is set before us so that we may embrace it.

In John 15:5, the scriptures tell us that without Him, we can do nothing. These many truths are set before believers so they may fully embrace and seek out the Lord while He may be found. These are words from the Lord that we have no option but to obey, to fully seek after so that we may embrace the Christ. Doing this will not only save us but also allow us to reach out to others as commissioned sons and daughters. We do have the gracious opportunity to repent and return to our Lord Jesus Christ. The way and the pathway of the Lord is narrow and yet promising.

Chapter 14

Spiritual Worship

Every believer has God's authority to walk in Christ's victory. However, believe it or not, many evil spirits (disguised) lord over God's people. In other words, the souls of human beings need to be restored, transformed, and lifted from the hands of Satan and his disguised captivity. So, if you are in the pit of unforgiveness, hurt, or emotional trauma, get out of that demonic pit and move forward. Joseph was hurt but did not remain in the pit—and you don't have to either. Such is not God's order. The human soul having dominion over the spirit is a violation of God's creation order.

The sons and daughters of God have been mandated to achieve 100 percent obedience according to the scriptures (1 Thessalonians 5:23–24). It's time to cry out for God's will. Jesus said, "The hour cometh, and now is, when the true worshipper shall worship the Father in spirit and in truth. For the Father seeks such to worship him. God is spirit, and they that worship him must worship him in spirit and in truth" (John 4:23–24).

Soulish Worship

Loud noises do not make for spiritual worship. Soulish worship is habitually disguised as demonic noise with loud musical instruments, amplifiers, keyboards, excessive loud drums, and so forth, all of which offends the Father. We must abandon these ways and come to know Him in spirit and truth. Most believers know this is a fact but are too lethargic to achieve it in their worship practices. The Father says, "Search the Scriptures; for in them ye think you have eternal life: and it is they that bear witness to me" (John 5:39). This message is for all God's sons and daughters. Since we are standing on the promises of God, let us encourage one another to reach out to please the Lord. "You shall know the truth and the truth shall make you free" (John 8:32), even from the controlling works of darkness.

Unforgiveness

The behavior of unforgiveness is a hidden and entrenched enemy in the soul of many believers. A good example is the many leaders who are hard of heart (i.e., living in pride and resentment) against certain believers whom they regard as second class. I have observed these attitudes, and it was my job to pray for those people who exhibited them.

It is time to cry out to Jesus and confront this reality because you have been called to God's freedom. Again, get out of the pit of your past. Only Christ can effectively remove the evil presence and habitual behavior from your life. Since Satan is the accuser of the brethren, you need to cry out for divine help from our almighty Father. Bad behavior and gross disrespect for the church or ministry must be avoided because you are called to be holy as He is holy. In spite of God's Word, it is not appropriate to continue to blame others (i.e., make false accusations) because of the hardness of one's heart. It is time to cry out to the Father to expel the fraudulent works of darkness from the soul. There are evil spirits that attempt to stop God's work by performing stealth activities within the body of Christ. Often these spirits of envy, jealousy, and strife attempt to invade a church and cause havoc. "O Lord my God, I cried unto thee, and thou hast healed me. O Lord thou hast brought up my soul from the grave: thou hast kept me alive, that I should not go down to the pit" (Psalm 30:2–3).

My observations about the body of Christ have shown me that this is a major issue. This demonic problem seems to affect a large part of the body of Christ in two ways: (1) The damaging effects are not taught from the pulpit, and (b) many believers do not believe or know about the ingrained negative effects of unforgiveness that are hiding in their souls. The evil content that lies in the soul is not from heaven; rather, it is a carnal deposit from the workers of iniquity.

Spiritual Foundation. Responsibility of Church Leadership

The church of God is built upon God's authority. According to the revelation found in Matthew 16:18, "And I say also unto thee, that thou art Peter, and upon this rock I will build my church; and the gates of hell shall not prevail against it. And I will give unto thee the keys of the kingdom of heaven." Every spiritual leader of Christ's church, for example, the pastors, elders, and teachers of God's Word, is anointed and commissioned by the Father to enlighten all believers with the bread of life (Jesus Christ) sent from heaven (John 6:51).

Again, only the powerful Word of God is well able to restore the soul and deliver the body, which happens after the salvation of your spirit, when it is joined to the Holy Spirit. The Father's creation order must not be violated; God said that it is the spirit, the soul, and the body, in this order. Any other order is complete rebellion against the authority of the Father's Word. Remember, if there is unforgiveness in your soul, Satan knows it. A person who harbors unforgiveness is driven by Satan to hurt others, believing wrongly that he or she may take advantage of others. Many times Satan uses the carnal mind to falsely accuse innocent believers without any evidence!

Chapter 15

Our Assigned Journey

God's purpose and plan for believers is foremost. As we take part in our assigned pilgrimage, the Holy Spirit will continue to reveal His boundless plan for us, the sons and daughters of God. Since we are in Christ, the apostle Paul states, "For through him we both have access by one Spirit unto the Father. Now therefore ye are no more strangers and foreigners, but fellow citizens with the saints, and of the household of God; and are built upon the foundation of the apostles and prophets, Jesus Christ himself being the chief corner stone; in whom all the building fitly framed together growth unto an holy temple in the Lord. In whom ye also are built together for a habitation of God through the Spirit" (Ephesians 2:18–22 ESV).

We are a habitation of God, His holy temple, as we live in the process of being changed into His image and likeness. To be changed into His likeness, the soul and the body must be targeted and transformed. Permanence must be the focus of true sons and daughters to ensure this is timely accomplished in Him. Our desire must be keenly focused on Christ as we journey to come forth in His likeness and image.

Continuation of our assigned journey is not an option; "seek ye the kingdom of God" is foremost. All this must come to us by His spiritual revelation. "But we all, with open face beholding as in a glass the glory of the Lord, are changed into the same image from glory to glory, even as by the Spirit of the Lord" (2 Corinthians 3:17).

His Purpose and Plan Is Foremost

In our journey in Christ "we are delivered unto spiritual death for Jesus sake, that the life also of Jesus might be made manifest in our mortal flesh" (2 Corinthians 4:11). We are His earthen vessels destined to be like Christ, but the soul and flesh must progressively be transformed, and spiritually we must die and be raised up as His resurrection unfolds in His sons and daughters. The spirit of resurrection dwells in our mortal bodies as it dwelled in Christ. This is the great plan that our Father has made, including the provisions for His sons and daughters to be like Him as ambassadors on earth. We are called to rule and reign on earth; therefore the gift of righteousness must flood our hearts, thus enabling us sons and daughters to function and have a prosperous Christlike relationship with one another. It is said in 2 Corinthians 4:7, "But we have this treasure in clay jars, so that it may be made clear that this extraordinary power belongs to God and does not come from us" (ESV).

As we are in Christ, our major goal is to be fully restored and to operate in the unconditional love of God, namely, the agape spirit. Again, the Father has spiritually targeted the soul and flesh of believers with many scriptures to achieve His purpose in the lives of His people (spirit, soul, and body/flesh).

Let us consider and embrace the innumerable scriptures that the Father continues to use to target the soul and flesh of His sons and daughters for the express concern of purification and restoration. Again, this progressive purification progress is *meant to deliver the sons and daughters of God into the Father's image and likeness.* God has granted the anointed minister of God to use His keys (authority) to bring forth the intended greatness of blessings to promote His kingdom.

Seeking His Presence

It is the Father's pleasure to give salvation to all the believers the kingdom; therefore He has set the pathway for believers to travel. This is the pathway of the Holy Spirit. As Jesus suffered, so will God's sons and daughters suffer. However, the Father's rewards are great and promising! In other words, keep your eyes on the great and precious promises:

- "Beloved, I pray that in all respects you may prosper and be in good health, just as your soul (mind, will and desires) prospers" (3 John 1:3). Note: It is the Father's authority given to the believer that as the soul prospers, so will your health increase and be blessed.

- "In humility receive the word implanted, which is able to save your souls" (James 1:21).
- "Obtaining the outcome of your faith the salvation of your souls" (1 Peter 1:9).
- "God of peace Himself sanctify you entirely and may *your spirit and soul and body* be preserved complete without blame at the coming of our Lord Jesus Christ" (1 Thessalonians 5:23; emphasis added).
- "He restores my soul; He leads me in the paths of righteousness for His name's sake" (Psalm 23:3 ESV).
- "The law of the Lord is perfect, restoring the soul" (Psalm 19:7).
- "To bring back his soul from the pit, that he may be enlightened with the light of life" (Job 33:30).
- "But we are not of them who draw back unto perdition; but them that believe to the saving of the soul" (Hebrews 10:39).

Joseph, Moses, David, and Paul effectively dealt with the spirit of unforgiveness. Therefore, you are enabled by the same resurrected spirit to overcome all manner of unforgiveness. Unforgiveness is a part of every believer's life; however, the ministers and the congregants have to overcome the spirit of unforgiveness. Each time this spirit arrives, the grace and mercies of God will enable you to overcome it.

What about you? Are you having issues of unforgiveness? Like ministers, congregants have to overcome unforgiveness. Therefore, the believer's responsibility is to pursue and achieve the purity of Christ only via forgiveness. Every believer will have some kind of encounter with the spirit of opposition; especially the spirit of unforgiveness will challenge every believer. Jesus experienced this, and so will you.

Chapter 16

Adamic Fallen Nature!

After Adam's sin (open eyes; not being deceived) in the garden; this sin affected the whole world. That is, the sin of one man had repercussions upon the whole word. The first Adam sinned, and the second Adam died and was resurrected to bring life to a condemned world. My intentions to show how one man's affected the whole world; but God's man's Jesus Christ came to give opportunity for all to be restored.

The Apostle Paul's Cry

"But I see in my members another law at war with the law of my mind and making me captive to the law of sin which dwells in my members. Wretched man that I am! Who will deliver me from this body of death? Thanks be to God through Jesus Christ our Lord! So then, I of myself serve the law of God with my mind, but with my flesh I serve the law of sin" (Romans 7:23–25). "There is therefore now no condemnation for those who are in Christ Jesus. For the law of the Spirit of life in Christ Jesus has set me free from the law of sin and death" (Romans 8:2).

We are living in a *fallen/sinful/destructive world* in response to the first Adamic nature. In my experience, the church's worship service is too often soulish (nonspiritual), including the preaching, the teaching, and the worship song compositions. With loud music, loud drums, and screaming voices, there is no evidence of Christ's presence. Many times the dancing is not of the way of Christ, ending a fleshly dance with intense screaming. Walking through the congregation to incite others to dance is not appropriate. I have seen extremes that are very offensive to me.

Evil Deception Is Often Alive and Active in Worship Services

This happens because of the lack of spiritual teaching of the Father's Word. The enemy is walking about as a roaring lion, seeking whom he may devour, even those among the body of Christ. The soulish spirit knows how to camouflage itself to bring about deception or false worship. We are expressly mandated to worship the Lord in spirit and in truth. This mandate is not an option but is the expressed will of the Father. The enemy knows how to conceal himself in false worship, and such is not pleasing to the Lord.

Paul tells us that as preachers and teachers in the church we are to feed (with the bread of life) the lambs as well as the sheep. John 6:51 says, "I am the living bread which came down from heaven: if any man eats of this bread, he shall live forever; and the bread that I will give is my flesh, which I will give for the life of the world is my flesh." Paul further validates this fact when he says, "And how shall they hear without a preacher? And how shall they preach, except they be sent?" (Romans 10:14). "The words that we must preach are that which brings life" (John 6:63).

Chapter 17

The Father's Grace: The Ultimate Answer to a Fallen World

To Him Who Knows to Do Good but Does Not Do It

We are no longer our own, for surely we have been bought with a great price: Christ sacrificed for the believer, paid the great price, died for us, and was resurrected at the point of water baptism on the third day. We have many witnesses to this great sacrifice so that we might live and not die.

Spiritually we are dead with Him yet alive with the Father upon becoming one with Him. Romans 6:7–8 says, "For he that is [spiritually—spirit, soul, and body] dead is freed from sin. Now if we be dead with Christ, we believe that we shall also live with him." God's powerful resurrected Spirit now connects His Son's Spirit with us so that progressive relationship and fellowship may be achieved. Romans 6:5–6 reminds us: "For if we have been planted together in the likeness of his death, we shall be, also in the likeness of his resurrection: knowing this, that our old man is crucified with him, that the body of sin might be destroyed that henceforth we should not serve sin." Romans 6:7 says, "For he that is dead is freed from sin."

That is the only way to get free from sin—to die to it (which requires humility and prayer). Death does not mean only extinction. It also means extinction of life in Christ or to be separated from God, meaning a physical death. God said, "Separate yourself from this thing. Die to it." If we are spiritually dead with Christ, we believe that we shall also spiritually live with Him. Water baptism is the signification of this truth. When you go down in the waters of baptism, your Adamic nature, your carnal nature, is submerged in the water. When you are covered by the waters, it means you are spiritually buried. When you come up out of the waters of baptism, your spirit is resurrected in Christ (spiritually) (1 Peter 3:21–22). Though you probably have experienced this milestone firsthand, I discuss it here to remind you of its meaning and importance.

Dead to Sin

The apostle Paul addresses this fact in Romans 6:1–4: "What shall we say then? Shall we continue in sin that grace may abound? God forbids. How shall we, that are dead to sin, live any longer therein? Know ye not, that so many of us as were baptized into Jesus Christ were baptized into his death? *Therefore, we are buried with him by baptism into death: that like as Christ was raised up from the dead by the glory of the of the Father, even so we also should walk in newness of life*" (emphasis added).

Chapter 18

God's Perfection: Internal Reformation, the Born-Again Experience

Remember that Paul said, "I die daily" (1 Corinthians 15:31). That old nature will rise up again and again, and at such times you have to determine (by power of the Word) who will be king of your life (Romans 1:16). Our focus on the King, Christ Jesus, must be given preeminence at all times. Furthermore, we must embrace Christ in our daily pursuits. Matthew 6:33 reminds us, "Seek you first the kingdom of God and His righteousness and God will add all things to His Sons."

If you are an irritated person every day (with a spirit of depression), then your soulish part is the boss of your life. If you falsely say, "I'm grieved. I'm sad," hallelujah! It's a new day. Perhaps a lying spirit has overtaken you (1 Kings 22:23; 2 Chronicles 18:21).

The spirit part of you—the Christ, our hope of glory (charity, agape)—will become great in your life. Be reminded: "But put ye on the Lord Jesus Christ and make not provision for the flesh to fulfill the lusts thereof" (Romans 13:14). "For I delight in the law of God after the inward man: But I see another law in my members, warring (spiritual warfare) against the law of my mind and bringing me into captivity to the law of sin which is in my members" (Romans 7:22–23).

The soul of a human being, especially in its unregenerate state, is in a state of rebellion against the person's spirit; plus, it violates the creation order. This controversy between spirit and soul includes such things as resentment, emotional hurts, self-pity, and self-defeat (Romans 8:7).

The soul of a person must be the servant of the spirit. All independent actions, which have to do with thinking, feeling, and deciding, must surrender (yield) to the "born again spirit of man," For as many that are led by the Spirit are the sons of God. [Rom 8:14.] There are millions of Christians walking around feeling condemned, depressed, and angry right now, and it's a soulish-emotional problem. The reason for feeling such a way is that the soul (emotions) is overly dominated by an evil spirit. Many spirits come with an accusing spirit, and if it feels true, then the weak one accepts it as fact. The question here is, Which report will you believe, the report of the Lord or the report of your feelings? Romans 8:1 says, "There is therefore now no condemnation to them which are in Christ Jesus. Who do not walk according to the flesh, but according

65

to the Spirit?" The apostle Paul is saying here that many believers are angry because of the different matters of life and never overcome this anger. Even Dr. Stanley says in his book, "Too many believers attending church are angry for many different reasons!"

The human soul is the old creation, the Adamic fallen nature. The word *soul* comes from *psyche*, from which is derived the word *psychology*. The soul does not originate from the born-again supernatural nature that God places within us. God's creation order is the spirit first, the soul next, and the body last. Therefore, the Holy Spirit only communicates with the spirit of humankind and not the soul of humankind. First Corinthians 2:14 says, "But the natural man (soul and body) receiveth not the things of the Spirit of God: for they are foolishness unto him." You have a conflict with your soulish parts (Adamic nature) wanting to dominate or overpower your spiritual parts.

Paul tells us in Romans that we have to conduct spiritual warfare until we subdue these soulish issues. Your soul's Adamic nature will laugh at your born-again spirit. This soulish nature is enmity (carnal mind) toward God. Cry out in prayer: "Bring that powerful spiritual born-again nature into the Son and revive the spirit part of the believer." Call upon Him; His holy presence with the Word will come into your mind, feelings, and emotions, and you will progressively become a new person in the Lord Jesus Christ. *This is the born-again experience or, better said, the Nicodemus experience.*

Cry Out for Change: The Inward Person

At birth, you received a fallen nature. Such a nature opposes any form of the Holy One, which is resident in the soul of humankind. Now these are the three basic areas of your soul: mind, will, and emotions. This is the real you at that moment you are born. This soulish area is certainly not right until these areas are restored and resurrected by the Holy Spirit. Because of our previous emotions, feelings, bitterness, hurts, and thoughts, we need full restoration and constant renewal from the Holy Spirit.

Relationship Is Ongoing

Relationship is not an option, but the Father's mandate. There are four pillars that the believer must completely embrace: the Apostles' Doctrine, fellowship, the breaking of bread, and prayers. So the second pillar is relationship! This again is not an option but God's mandate. We learn in Acts 2:42, "They spent their time in learning from the apostles, taking part in the fellowship [*koinonia*—a relationship to share in]," and sharing in the fellowship means to pray. Although many events have occurred along this spiritual road, we believers must continue to pursue an ever-increasing high level of relationship with the Father. There are many benefits to a perpetual relationship with the Father. The greatest benefit is spoken to us by the apostle Paul: "pressing toward the mark for the prize of the high calling of God in Christ Jesus. Not that I have already attained, or am already perfected; but I press on, that I may lay hold of that for which Christ Jesus has also laid hold of me. Brethren, I do not count myself to have apprehended; but one thing I do, forgetting those things, which are behind, and reaching forward to those things which are ahead, I press toward the goal for the prize of the upward call of God in Christ Jesus" (Philippians 3:12–14).

Chapter 19

Reassurance: Confirmation by the Holy Spirit

One of the major keys is to urge the believer within the body of Christ to fully embrace Christ's presence. The prophet Isaiah said, "No weapon that is formed against thee shall prosper; and every tongue that shall rise against thee in judgment thou shalt condemn. This is the heritage of the servants of the Lord and their righteousness is of me, saith the Lord" (Isaiah 54:17).

Increased Demonic Activity / Evil Oppositions

The following are things to do at times when you experience increased demonic activity and evil opposition:

Sing a Song

Regarding wickedness and violence invading the house of God, and gross disrespect for one another even to the point of false accusations, David strongly advises the believer to sing a song in the night season. He knew what a night season was like when his and Bathsheba's baby died. He repented and went into immediate fasting. "Thou art my hiding place; thou shalt preserve me from trouble; thou shalt encompass me about with songs of deliverance. Selah" (Psalm 32:7). This is the psalmist's advice to fight the good fight of faith in order to maintain a high level of joy. In His presence is the fullness of joy. Again, this is the Father's precious and great promise for His family, the body of Christ.

Start Rejoicing

Two of God's faithful servants fully demonstrated the true fight for victory. They are King David and God's anointed Smith Wigglesworth, a British evangelist. Smith Wigglesworth never asks Smith Wigglesworth how he feels. What in the world does he mean? He is saying the same thing that David said in Psalm 42:11: "Why art thou cast down, O my soul, rejoice thou in the Lord." David was talking to David. The spirit man David was talking to the soulish man David, saying, "David, you get up out of that gutter, stop being sad, and start rejoicing in the Lord. Get busy. Rejoice in Jehovah." Physical encouragement, counseling, and support are always important, but the individual is called to be willing and obedient. Yes, David experienced some depression, but he found his way out of depression via his praising of the Father for His greatness. The Holy Spirit will override the works of darkness and even give you a song in the night season!

Chapter 20

Acquisitions of Knowledge: Message for Kings, Oracles of the Word of God

Knowledge by Revelation

To become a king or a priest, one must do as the Father commands—be led by the Spirit—as found in 1 Peter 4:11. The sons and daughters of God have been gifted, and we must continue to follow His leadership. As seen in 2 Corinthians 5:20, "Therefore, we are ambassadors for Christ, God making his appeal through us" (ESV). I implore you on behalf of Christ to be reconciled to God and live within His knowledge in spirit, soul, and body.

Another witness God gives to believers is found in 2 Peter 1:3–9:

> Confirm your calling and election; His divine
> power has granted to us all things that pertain to
> life and godliness, through the knowledge of Him

who called us to his own glory and excellence by which he has granted to us his precious and very great promises, so that through them you may become partakers of the divine nature, having escaped for the corruption that is in the world because of sinful desire. For this very reason, make every effort to supplement your faith with virtue, and virtue with knowledge, and knowledge with self-control, and self-control with steadfastness, and steadfastness with godliness, and godliness with brotherly affection with love. For if these qualities are yours and are increasing, they keep you from being ineffective or unfruitful in the knowledge of our Lord Jesus Christ. For whoever lacks these qualities is so nearsighted that he is blind, having forgotten that he was cleansed from his former sins. Finally, to him that knoweth to do good and do it not is sin!

So in my prayers I cry out that I may become obedient to our Father. This is how the believer grows and matures in the spirit, by yielding daily to the voice of the Father and daily building a relationship with the Father.

Peter's Plea. God Is Targeting Unredeemed Souls and Bodies

"Be diligent to confirm your calling and election, for if you practice these qualities you will never fall" (2 Peter 1:10–12 ESV). Here Peter is addressing the soul that the prophet Jeremiah addresses in Jeremiah 17:10. These gifted promises of God are filled with grace, mercy, and truth. The highway of holiness is there for God's people, given for their victorious journey (Isaiah 35:8). We are destined to reach Mount Zion as we progress and mature by overcoming countless trials and passing countless tests en route to becoming mature sons and daughters in Christ. The global picture is that the Father's purpose and His demands must be received, understood, and embraced in our hearts. Each of these varied experiences must be understood and received from the Father's hand because He is preparing us for a boundless future.

Our God Is Merciful and Graceful in All His Ways

He is the author and sender of corrections; however, we must be spiritually open to His tweaking of our hearts. These spiritual visitations from the Father should never be understood as rejections. Which are you going to believe, the soulish response or the Father's hand of correction? By having the mind of Christ, we are capable of receiving the necessary correction as we journey forward for His purpose. We must anticipate countless distractions during our journey back to the Father. Yes, we believers will encounter many distractions authored by Satan to change our minds. One man's intention was good, but a tragedy struck his family, and he decided to turn his back on God. Many get offended because of their misunderstanding, which may cause some to turn from God. "Because of this, many of Jesus' followers turned back and would not go with him anymore. So, he asked the twelve disciples, 'And you—would you also like to leave?'" (John 6:66–67 GNT). Again, Jonah did not follow the instructions of the Lord, so God laid up corrections for Jonah. Later, Jonah cried out to the Lord and began to obey Him.

Spirit-Filled Words

What about the soul and the body? Only by the spirit-filled Word does God cause change to come forth both internally and externally, bringing about in the believer a sacred transformation in Christ. The gospel of the kingdom must be preached to initiate internal change, according to John 6:63: "It is the *spirit that quickeneth; the flesh profiteth nothing*; the words that I speak unto you, they are spirit, and they are life" (emphasis added). When the anointed Word is preached, David says, "The law of the Lord is perfect (flawless), restoring and refreshing the soul; the statutes of the Lord are reliable and trustworthy, making wise the simple" (Psalm 19:7 AB). James says, "Receive with meekness the engrafted word, which is able to save your souls."

Regardless of how you approach the Word of God, only the gospel of the kingdom will bring the divine results of transformation and reformation (progressive salvation) to both your soul and body. There is divine power unto salvation in the preached Word of God to bring about this appointed internal change. There is a great need in the body of Christ from the pulpit to the pew as every person needs this purification through the gospel of Christ. This purification is not to be taken frivolously. The apostle Peter speaks of it in this way: "Seeing ye have purified your souls in obeying the truth through the Spirit unto unfeigned love of the brethren, see that ye love one another with a pure heart fervently" (1 Peter 1:22).

Great Redeemer

Our God is a truthful and redeeming Father who loves His people. We, the sons and daughters, have been called to come forth in His image and likeness. God's redemptive plan is laid upon and within His sons and daughters to cause them to grow, develop, and mature in the unity of His Spirit, making us one in Him. The work of the Holy Spirit is progressive in bringing about this envisioned freedom.

As I observe and think about professional and college football broadcasts, I notice that the officials use the term *targeting*, meaning an attack upon the opponent ball carrier's helmet (the unregenerate soul/flesh). This term rings a loud bell in my heart concerning *God's total plan for His people.* God is targeting every believer to develop spiritually to eventually progress and mature to be like Him. He has given us power to overcome all the works of darkness and deceptions of the enemy. The soul of a human being (in his or her humanity) must be the servant of the Spirit. This is the *Father's creation order*: (1)

the human spirit as the master, (2) the human soul as the servant, and (3) the human body as the slave.

There is a tremendous number of scriptures in which the Father targets the soul of His sons and daughters for His redemptive purposes. The soul and body of each believer has to be regenerated, restored, and crucified (Romans 7:23–24; Galatians 2:20). The Father has divine authority to call His sons and daughters for His purpose. Jonah went another way, but God had the final say over his life. Jonah did get it right after the Father sent correction his way. Those whom God calls sometimes resist. The Father's wisdom effectively targets the called so as to get the proper response.

Chapter 21

Lack of Knowledge: The Truth Will Set You Free

There are many reasons, excuses, and misunderstandings concerning having a knowledge of God's Word. One significant reason is the works of the enemy—warfare against the believers and nonbelievers alike to trigger darkness concerning the Word. For sure the carnal person, with Satan's efforts to deliver confusion to the body of Christ, has resulted in much deception. This evil work of Satan has confused many people in the body of Christ. The tradition of church elders and leaders has led them to interpret the Word of the Lord intellectually rather than giving them an understanding of God's Word. You must take the Word of God only as spoken by the Holy Spirit; otherwise, whose report are you going to believe? Further, God says that those who seek Him will find Him through His Word (Jeremiah 29:13).

Only the Holy Spirit can and will unscramble this problem. Matthew speaks of the key: "Blessed are those who hunger and thirst for righteousness, for they shall be satisfied" (Matthew 5:6). "Blessed are the pure in heart for they shall see God" (Matthew 5:8). Many church leaders have preached and taught God's Word, but too often they have given a different message of the Holy Spirit. The Holy Spirit is a great dynamic teacher of the Father's Word. His greatest desire to is to bring forth these truths into the hearts of His sons and daughters. God said that we should seek Him first (Matthew 6:33), and He will add the wisdom, knowledge, and understanding to bless is on our journey!

The writer of Hebrews 12:1 encourages the believer to follow Christ as the race of becoming one with the Father has been set before us. My sincere observation is that the body of Christ is not diligent enough to run in this appointed race. From the pulpit to the pew, church people seem to have lost their love, their righteous pathway, and their desire to run after Christ.

In Romans 8:18, Paul again speaks to believers, "For I reckon that the sufferings of this present time are not worthy to be compared with the glory which shall be revealed in us." In other words, there are spiritual rewards in Christ at the end of this race for the genuine sons and daughters of God. Who are the real sons and daughters? According to Romans 8:14, those who are led by the Spirit of God are the (genuine) sons and daughters of God.

At the same time, the Holy Spirit is beckoning us and saying to the whole of creation that "groaneth," awaiting the manifestation of the sons and daughters of God: "For we know that the whole creation groaneth and travaileth in pain together until now. And not only they, but ourselves also, which have the first fruits of the Spirit, even we ourselves groan within ourselves, waiting for the adoption, to wit, the redemption of our body" (Romans 8:19–23).

Chapter 22

Goodness of the Father: The Power of Salvation

The apostle Paul said, "For I am not ashamed of the gospel of Christ: for it is the power of God unto salvation to everyone that believeth; to the Jew first, and also to the Greek. For therein is the righteousness of God revealed from faith to faith as it is written. The just shall live by faith" (Romans 1:16–17).

By faith this must be dealt with in a way of understanding, even knowing the other written letters of the word, who express their insight into unregenerate behavior and the concerns of the soul. The soul of humankind is actually the center and the core of the human personality; such as emotions, including the part that is seductive, deceiving, seeking in self-interest, and craving for carnal gratification. If you're a born-again believer joined to the Holy Spirit, then He will enable you to overcome any form of satanic darkness that habitually dwells in the soulish parts of your being. Remember, Paul said, "O wretched man that I am! who shall deliver me from the body of this death?" (Romans 7:24).

There are numerous scriptures that speak to the works of darkness and the wickedness of the forces of darkness. Second Timothy 1:7 reveals the evil activities of the unregenerate soul. The heart (unregenerate soul) is full of evil. "It is what comes out of a person that makes him unclean. For from the inside, from a person's heart, come the evil ideas which lead him to do immoral things, to rob, kill, commit adultery, be greedy, and do all sorts of evil things; deceit, indecency, jealousy, slander pride, and folly—all these evil things come from inside a person and make him unclean" (Mark 7:21–23).

Who Can Know the Heart of Humankind?

Only the Father knows the contents and characteristics of the human heart. Therefore, the Holy Spirit enables one another to demonstrate the true and genuine love for one another. The prophet Jeremiah addresses this fact: "The heart is deceitful above all things, and desperately wicked, who can know it?" (Jeremiah 17:9). So, confession is in order for every believer because the Father has a great desire to bestow His grace upon His sons and daughters. He said, "Blessed are the pure in heart, for they shall see God, our Father." The Word of God has come to bless and establish every believer so that they all effectively have their eyes open to God's dreams and visions.

As you begin to embrace various appointed revelations from the Father, you will realize more inner harmony and even greater harmony in your relationships with others. The following is a critical scripture: "I the Lord search the mind and try the heart, to give to every man according to his ways, according to the fruit of his doings" (Jeremiah 17:10).

The Father's Heart—Lovely Dwellings

As we examine this particular scripture, it is my intention to look beyond the faults of the people and see Christ, the hope of promoting individual people to be like their Maker (God); our Maker is love, light, peace, and redemption. Our thought lives and feelings are not always reassuring and do not always express care for one another. This is just like Christ, who did not please Himself. But as it is written, "The reproaches of those who reproached thee fell upon Me" (Romans 15:3 ESV). Christ has made provisions, giving us an example of a disciplined thought life (helmet of salvation) as described in Ephesians 6:12. Paul said, "Put ye on, concerning putting forth of the spiritual armor of God." The part that protects our thought lives is the helmet of salvation.

We are charged as the sons and daughters of God to have the mind of Christ. Having the mind of Christ requires full dedication and a strong commitment to follow on to know the Lord. One thing that's important to have is a dedicated and vibrant relationship with your spiritual family as well as with outsiders. "Do not merely look out for your own personal interests, but also for the interests of others. Have this same attitude (mind) in yourselves which was in Christ Jesus" (Philippians 2:4–5 ESV). In selfless humility, look to Him as your example of God's unfolding development of His more excellent Word.

The writer of Hebrews 12:28 says, "Wherefore, *we are receiving a kingdom which cannot be moved*, let us have grace, whereby we may serve God acceptably with reverence and godly fear" (emphasis added). I sense not only that God is calling His sons and daughters to an abundant lifestyle but also that the heart (spirit, soul, and body) of His people must be sanctified as His presence abides internally, thus comforting the believers. This is the abundant life that's offered and clearly promised to the sons and daughters of God. He is a Father of delightful fellowship (koinonia—to share in), and He so desires to build a great relationship with His sons and daughters because He ordained fellowship to be His second pillar as listed in Acts 2:42, about the apostolic ministry.

For sure our definition of God's love and care for us must be reworked and fully understood, which comes about only by the cross. Because we know that whomever God loves, He chastens (in His graceful redemptive love) for His purpose to bring about change so that the person may be accepted into His kingdom. This change has to do with the mind of the soul and the mind of the body. It is true that when God chastens, it is not rejection (never to be misunderstood) but is, rather, redemptive correction.

"For whom the Lord loveth he chasteneth [expression of redemptive love and care] and scourgeth [punishes] every son whom he receiveth. If ye endure chastening, God dealeth with you, as with sons; for what son is he whom the father chasteneth not?" (Hebrews 12:6–7 NKJV). If there are others who are disobedient and disrespectful, *punishment is inevitable.* Sometimes your privileges are cut or terminated for a period of time; some may even experience something as severe as removal from a particular office. God determines the appropriate punishment for each point of sin. To have an understanding of these distinctions is to reflect the mind of Christ Jesus. It is very important to understand the difference between chastening the sons and daughters and punishing the disobedient.

Two concerns are that the soul must be properly approached and changed by the purifying Word of God (Ephesians 5:26). Both the soul and the body have to be properly dealt with according to the Spirit of God. There is much beauty in redemptive brokenness, which is designed to bring us to the ultimate level of divine relationship with the Holy Father. A great example is Joseph, who was sold and, in the end, brought restoration to his family. It was a beautiful time of complete restoration after such a long period. Just as Jesus was broken on the cross at Calvary, being our example, we must be broken as well. I will say again, in order to prepare each son or daughter to reach that heavenly plateau, the merciful hands of Jesus are required.

It is the Father's desire to have a family of sons and daughters as His earthly ambassadors (the body of Christ) who are in His likeness and image. It is a fact that we are not all clean, and there is much work to be done in our hearts (souls), based solely on many encounters dispatched from His hand. These timely encounters are designed to keep His sons and daughters focused on and steadfast to his purpose and destiny. In the eyes of the Lord, He sees fellowship among His sons and daughters, a close relationship to bring them into His body as true sons and daughters. A true relationship and genuine fellowship is the true definition of progressive salvation pertaining to the spirit, soul, and body.

Chapter 23

Refiner's Fire: Christ Is Your Source

The prophet Isaiah uttered these words: "For mine eyes are upon all their ways; they are not hiding from my face, neither is their iniquity hid from mine eyes." It is the Father's stated desire to rid His people of every iniquity by way of the "refiner's fire." Mal. 3:3 KJV. Isaiah said, "He was bruised for our iniquities:" Further, "I, the Lord, search the heart, I try the reins, even to give every man according to his ways, and according to the fruit of his doings." This relationship calls for each believer to seek after the Lord as he speaks of King Uzziah: "And he sought God in the days of Zechariah, who had understanding in the visions of God; and as long as he sought the Lord, God made him to prosper" (2 Chronicles 26:5).

I personally believe that the key to prosperity in Christ is to seek Him day and night coupled with meditation. One must spend time in His presence, meditating, singing, reading the Word, and engaging in much intercessory prayer. "This book of the Law shall not depart out of thy mouth; but thou shalt meditate therein day and night, that thou mayest observe to do according to all that is written therein; for then thou shalt make thy way prosperous, and then thou shalt have good success" (Joshua 1:8–9). In view of these Words of God, we must be filled with the Holy Spirit so that we may also be enabled and empowered to overcome the evil wishes of the unregenerate soul and the works of the flesh. As we read in Luke 12:31, "But rather seek ye the kingdom of God; and all these things shall be added unto you."

Called to Relationship

Again, Joshua tells us to meditate day and night. Surely, we can make our way prosperous by the power of God's Word. Therefore, our way in Christ is to seek and honor Him daily because the devil, our adversary, is walking about, seeking whom he may devour. It is of paramount importance to acknowledge the Lord Jesus. Then He will direct the paths of the righteous. With this direction, there is power and God's authority to achieve the ordained objectives. Jesus called His disciples to walk after Him and obey the principles of the kingdom.

Remember, He is our King and we are forever victorious disciples in Christ. Seek ye first the kingdom of God and His righteousness, and He will add to our lives with His divine abundance since He promised to supply our every need according to His riches in glory.

Therefore, our daily efforts to grow in Christ include an admonishment that we "be sober, be vigilant because [our] adversary, the Devil, as a roaring lion, walketh about seeking whom he may devour." [I Pet.5:8].

Distractions and Delays

For sure there will be opposition along our authorized journey because such demonic distractions, ill-activities, trials, and storms will enable our faith to fully develop and mature, which will grant us the breakthrough. Take courage and do not give in to the distractions that sometimes may even delay your achieving of your assigned goal. "Resist him, steadfast in the faith, know that the same afflictions are accomplished in your brethren that are in the world" (1 Peter 5:8–9). Remember, you are not alone in your fiery trials and tests. The greater purpose for these difficult periods is to promote you to higher level of leadership and authority in the kingdom of God. Is it time for your promotion?

God's Kingdom

There is a great need for consecrated and committed mature sons and daughters to come forth in His image and likeness. We are on the grace-based road to a refined relationship, an increased understanding of the Word, increased authority in the Word, and the knowledge that God is our Father and we are His sons and daughters.

There is no compromising in Christ because the spirit, soul, and body are in total submission to Christ, prepared for the future and now blameless at His coming. This is the promise that He has placed before us and within us because the Father loves His sons and daughters.

Chapter 24

Stay on the Path: The Holy Spirit Alone Is Your Appointed Director

Spiritual warfare is critical and vital for success; therefore, God gives leaders the ability to help the congregant stay the course and keep his or her focus on deliverance/freedom. Again, our spiritual journey is precious because the Father has placed this assignment into the hearts of His anointed sons (*huios*) and daughters. This is a major point that must be highlighted for those who are journeying in the Father's name. First, your journey requires continuous focus with an energetic relationship because of the varied and numerous distractions that will eventually confront you. There are many glamorous forms of temptations, glittering attractions that can fill your soul and mind with excuses, thus causing you to lose your focus.

The psalmist says, "Many are the afflictions of the righteous, but the Lord delivers us out of them all." It's the Father's mandate that we fight the good fight of faith, keeping the vision and the promise before us that the Father has covenanted with the believer. As the Hebrews writer states, "Looking unto Jesus, who is the author and finisher of our faith." Isaiah said, "The Lord is exalted; for he dwelleth on high: he hath filled Zion with judgment and righteousness." Therefore, God's presence is there to direct your pathway, for in His presence is the fullness of joy!

Trusting God: The Promise

As we progress toward spiritual Mount Zion, our eyes, as well as His eyes, are upon God's purpose and His goal to fulfill His promise. I have two witnesses here: Peter says, "The Lord is not slack concerning his promise, as some men count slackness; but is long-suffering to toward us, not willing that any should perish, but that all should come to repentance" (2 Peter 3:9). Jeremiah says, "'I say this because I know what I am planning for you,' says the Lord. 'I have good plans for you, not plans to hurt you. I will give you hope and a good future.'" We are in a spiritual covenant with God, who is our strength from day to day.

Our love for the Father is our God-given gift and our authority to follow on to know the Lord. Knowing the Lord involves more than just words; we strive lawfully to achieve the highest level of relationship and knowing (*epignosis*—intimate knowing) our covenant Father. The prophet Jeremiah said, "And ye shall seek me, and find me, when you shall search for me with all your heart. I will be found of you saith the Lord; I will turn away your captivity, and I will gather you from all the nations and the places whither I have driven you, saith the Lord" (Jeremiah 29:13–14).

Only by Revelation—Know the Father

As Paul stated, "That I may know him, and the power of his resurrection, and the fellowship of his sufferings, by becoming like him unto his death" (Philippians 3:10 ESV). He is addressing obtaining the knowledge of spiritual mysteries as inherent in the Greek word *gnosis*. Every sincere believer's cry is, "That I may know him!"

Chapter 25

Reaching Forth:
A Higher Calling

Paul Says, "Stay Awake"

Keep the purpose of your heart at the forefront. This will bring about acceleration or momentum; we must follow on to know Christ, which is the critical part in our relationship. As a warning, some situations bring some serious offenses, but your crying out to God will protect you and cover you with grace and mercy. "Forgetting what lies behind and straining toward what lies ahead, I press on toward the goal for the prize of the upward call of God in Christ Jesus" (Philippians 3:13–14 NKJV). We cannot afford to be distracted or go off course or out of relationship. Instead the believer must be watchful in all things, endure afflictions, do the work of an evangelist, and fulfill his or her ministry. Dedicated discipleship is very necessary and critical for our success. We are told to endure difficulty as good soldiers of Jesus Christ.

The appointed journey that is set before us is extremely challenging and testing for sure. We know that it's a fact that our souls, hearts, and minds must be purged, purified, and restored (Psalm 23:3). As we gain momentum, I believe that the joy of the Lord gives us that extra boost, the strength and resilient faith that will be our main carriers of success as we strive to attain our goal. The prophet Isaiah confirms this: "He giveth power to the faint; and to them that have no might he increaseth strength" (Isaiah 40:29).

Christ's Soldiers

In the midst of spiritual warfare, we are strongly advised to be strong in grace provided in Christ Jesus because we are called to endure difficulties as good soldiers of Jesus Christ. This difficulty is defined in terms of suffering, the encountering of many afflictions, and most of all, having a similar experience as Christ. Such opposition will help the believer to maintain a stronger focus on the task(s) at hand. However, God's grace is there to enable His soldiers to be successful in the midst of trials and tests ("I will never leave you nor forsake you"). Only through Christ are we well able to be supported in the midst of afflictions and hardships. This anointing enables the sons and daughters of God to be established and spiritually positioned as His earthly representatives.

Having done all to stand, we know that the many afflictions that present themselves—being miserable, being tormented, or bearing adversity—do not make for an easy position for God's people; only by God's given grace are we able to stand in His Word. When we have the mind of Christ, God will enable us to move forward and remain victorious. Moving forward in Christ is a clear sign of progressive salvation.

Reigning in Christ

It is only by faith that the victory that is in Christ is deposited in the believer. "It is a faithful saying: For if we be dead with him, we shall also live with him" (2 Timothy 2:12 NKJV). In other words, the victory belongs to the Lord. Although we are victorious as the sons and daughters of God, every believer must continue to live a sacrificial life (tested by fiery trials—He is in the midst of it all), keeping the momentum by constantly seeking the face of Christ, by extended times of fasting or regular extended periods of meditation. Yes, these are perilous times in which terrifying, violent, wicked people are a threat to the lives of the righteous as well as their communities. In spite of the divine call to live holy, it seems that the restraint of Christ is a thing of the past. But we have been warned of these things: "This know also, that in the last days perilous times shall come. For men shall be lovers of their own selves, covetous, boasters, proud, blasphemers, disobedient to parents, unthankful, unholy, and the list goes on" (2 Timothy 3:1–5 NKJV).

Satanic Deceptions

There are many deceptions among us because of the refusal to accept and obey the Word; it is disobedience in that many sons and daughters are not doers of the Word. Even some believers tend to be soulish and are disappointing in their behavior because they wrongfully engage in many bad behaviors and because their soul-minds and body-minds are yet to be cleansed (the greatest sinful parasite is threefold: jealousy, envy, and strife). All unwanted behaviors, unwanted actions, and negative attitudes flow and manifest themselves. They flow out of the unredeemed soul and the flesh. Many in the body of Christ are very elegant and religiously polished, having a form of godliness but denying and disgracing the one who graces us.

Yes, we have been graced by our Father, but there must be a "cry out of the heart to know the Father" and come into full compliance with the spirit mind and the minds of the soul and body. From the pulpit to the pew, the Father wants to purify each dimension of the threefold nature—spirit, soul, and body—of our humanity. We must pursue the Lord and not become an offense before God.

Redemptive Father (Ephesians 1:17)

So God is receptive to your cry for repentance, which is unquestionably the heart of the Father. This is clearly demonstrated in the passage about the prodigal son (Luke 15:11) and even the spirit of Jezebel (Revelation 2:20).

The soul and the body of person cannot continue without the Father's giving attention to those areas to allow for repentance. Why is this? The Father gives His full attention to all three entities of a human being. Regardless of the mind and the intent of the prodigal son, God's love was demonstrated in His continuous love for His wayward son. Although the son had been blinded by the cares of this world, the Father's prayer was there with him in spite of the son's rebellious heart. This wayward heart was met purposely with a mighty famine in the land. This is another example of the unconditional love of God for His wayward sons and daughters (Luke 15:14 NKJV).

Reconciled Hearts (2 Corinthians 5:18)

God commanded reconciliation, while Satan urges deception among the weak vessels in the house of God. Revelation 2:20–23 reads, "But I have this against you, that you tolerate that woman Jezebel [creation order violated, soulish] who calls herself a prophetess and is teaching and seducing my servants to practice sexual immorality and to eat food sacrificed to idols. I gave her time to repent, but she refuses to repent of her sexual immorality. And I will strike her children dead. And all the churches will know that I am He who searches mind and heart, and I will give to each of you according to your works."

Such disrespectful, shameless activity and wanton disregard is an abomination before the heart of the Lord.

This is not the activity of the Holy Spirit. It is the ruthless effect of the teamwork between the soul and body that failed to be cleansed and purified by the Word of God. Believe it or not, many wounded soldiers in the house of the Lord continue to justify their hurts and retain their unforgiveness. In my best estimation of such activity, these souls have been wounded in the house of the Lord. Yet God will not compromise His standard of holiness. However, our Father does have countless ways of bringing redemption to the wicked. Their hearts are driven to find their own way and are forced to overlook any warning signs to establish their way (however, warnings come via dreams and visions and through the ministers of God).

It is extremely dangerous to abuse the grace of God as the Word of God offers many spiritual warnings about sinful and rebellious living. It is the love of God, who clearly offers us His way and standards of holiness. Jesus said unto His disciples, "I am the way, the truth, and the life: no man cometh unto the Father, but by me" (John 14:6).

Let me repeat this point. There is no compromising (no respecting of persons in Christ) in seeking the Lord because He and the Father are one. "If ye had known me, ye should have known my Father also: and from henceforth ye know him and have seen him" (John 14:7). To go contrary to God's plan to purify the heart is to be very obstinate and disrespectful. This is what defiles a person. In Matthew 15:18–20, this is confirmed: "But those things which proceed out of the mouth come forth from the heart; and they defile the man. For out of the heart proceed evil thoughts, murders, adulteries, fornications, thefts, false witness, blasphemies. These are the things which defile a man: but to eat with unwashed hands defileth not a man."

Cry Out Perfection

Following are sincere warnings. Take heed. *Submit yourself to God*:

- "Cry out to become hungry and thirsty for Him" (Matthew 5:6). The prayers of a righteous person avail much; therefore, to cry out to the Lord is the initial requirement for His presence.
- "Be ye doers of the Word" (James 1:23). The Father would have His sons and daughters practice the lifestyle of the Father, for example, to love one another and honor one another.
- "O Lord my God, I cried to thee for help, and thou hast healed me" (Psalm 30:2). God is well able to restore His servants or rescue them from situations not pleasing to Him.
- "O Lord, thou hast brought up my soul from Sheol, restored me to life from among those gone down to the Pit" (Psalm 30:3). In other words, God is one who responds to the desperate. David even mentioned that the Father rescues those who cry for help. He is faithful and willing to deliver a person from hurt, harm, and danger. God has great plans for all His people in spite of

their wrongdoings! He rescued David; He rescued Joseph from the pit. He is no respecter of persons; His love is there for all of us.

Selfishness Offends

Although the soul of a human being is very keen, intelligent and prideful, such evil spirits must be in submission to the Holy One of Israel. Satan's intent is to make the soul of a human being superior to the spirit, but the Father's authority places the soul of a human being into a lesser position of being subject to the spirit. This is the Father's creation order: first the spirit, then the soul, and then the body. In other words, the spirit of pride attempts to oppose the principles and statutes of the kingdom of God.

The power and the abilities of the soul of the human being must not be destroyed, but rather this entity must be transformed, restored, and renewed in Christ. Only by the power of God's Word is humankind useful to the kingdom of God. In John 15:5 it says, "Apart from me, you can do nothing."

Remember, King Saul was a man who began in the spirit. We read in 1 Samuel 13:13–14: "And Samuel said to Saul, thou hast done foolishly: thou hast not kept the commandment of the Lord thy God which he commanded thee: for now, would the Lord have established thy kingdom upon Israel forever." But now thy kingdom shall not continue Jehovah hath sought him a man after his own heart."

When you live life dominated by your soulish parts, the Bible says you are living foolishly and have no respect for the directed pathway of the Father. Your Adamic fallen nature is insubordinate to the redeemed human spirit and the Spirit of God's Word.

Chapter 26

Victorious Churches

Victory in Christ!

"Now thanks be unto God, which always causeth us to triumph in Christ and make manifest the savor of his knowledge by us in every place. But thanks be to God, who gives us the victory through our Lord Jesus Christ" (1 Corinthians 15:57). As it was foretold by the prophet Isaiah, "He will not break a bruised reed or quench a smoldering wick, till he brings justice to victory" (Matthew 12:20). There is always victory in Jesus Christ because He is ever with His sons and daughters; therefore, there is no defeat in Him.

The Syrophoenician Woman (Mark 7:26–30)

Symbolically, this woman represents the church, the bride of Christ. The first woman who was an overcomer[3] came upon the church and heard embarrassing words meant to turn her away without her requested blessings. However, she was steadfast in her heart and stood with great expectations. Furthermore, she represents an overcoming church that refuses to give up as she demonstrated steadfastness in her faith. Another dimension is that she represents the *bride of Christ* in the price she had to pay to arrive at such a spiritual plateau in the kingdom of God. We are told to endure difficulty as good soldiers of Jesus Christ. Only the Lord can define this difficulty because He knows our capacity. Other words, only the Father knows our abilities to overcome trials and tests. [I Cor 10:13].

Woman with the Issue of Blood (Matthew 9:20–22; Mark 7:26)

The second woman who was an overcomer was the woman who suffered for eighteen years (three sixes—the spirit, soul, and body) with an issue of blood. Strong faith is critical to achieving the victory sought after. Jesus turned around, and when He saw her, He said, "Be of good cheer, daughter; your faith has made you well. And the woman was made well from that hour."

---

[3] An overcomer is one who has experienced victory over the works of darkness. "But thanks be to God who gives us the victory through our Lord Jesus Christ" (1 Corinthians 15:57 GNT)!

The Bent-Over Woman
(Mark 5:25–34; Luke 8:43)

The third young woman, being Jairus's daughter, was an overcomer too. This was the woman who was bent for twelve years. First, this woman had blood issues and was in a danger of losing her life because of blood loss. Her urgency was to gain life and be made whole by Jesus Christ. Second, the number 12 is a very important symbol in the kingdom of God. This number is a symbol of the government of God and the authority of the holy Father.

"But when Jesus heard it, He answered, saying, 'Do not be afraid; only believe, and she will be made well.' When He came into the house, He permitted no one to go in except Peter, James and John, and the father and mother of the girl. Jesus said, 'Little girl, arise.' Then her spirit returned, and she arose immediately" (Luke 8:50–55).

As I discuss the issues of a carnal church (one operating in the soul and flesh), lawlessness, undetected, invades the church. Too often, unqualified ministers and deacons carry out their spiritual duties with a carnal mind, disregarding the standards of holiness. False partakers are not accepted (Acts 8:18). Remember that the Word of God stands. "God is a Spirit: they that worship Him, shall worship Him in Spirit and in Truth" (John 4:24). Satan's tactic is discerned and repented of, then he is commanded to leave in Jesus's name.

The loving, forgiving, and redemptive Father will find ways to offer redemption to a rebellious people (Ephesians

1:7; Colossians 1:14). Remember, "But God will not take away life, and He devises means so that the banished one will not remain an outcast" (2 Samuel 14:14). There is hope in Christ that is laid out for all rebellious and backslidden people because Christ is graceful, full of mercy, and available to give hope to the hearts of His people.

Chapter 27

Transformation: Soul and Flesh

Again, it's all about spiritually dying and giving your full life to Christ. Paul said, "I was put to death on the cross with Christ, and I do not live anymore; it is Christ who lives in me" (Galatians 2:20). "I still live in my body, but I live by faith in the Son of God who loves me and gave himself to save me" (Galatians 2:20 NCV).

The threefold being is given to us; therefore, we have been commanded to be blameless at the appearing of Christ. Furthermore, the Father promised to help us achieve that level of purity (1 Thessalonians 5:23–24). To reinforce this fact, the Father promised to establish His sons and daughters and keep them from the evil one (2 Thessalonians 3:3). This is the standard of God our Father; now may God Himself, the God of peace, make you pure, belonging only to Him. May your whole self— spirit, soul, and body—be kept safe and be found to be without fault when our Lord Jesus comes again. You can trust the one who calls you to that transformation.

To aid in your understanding, I have given you three diagrams showing how our salvation is progressive and how it takes time for us to be completely redeemed (see Appendix B: Salvation Is Progressive). The Father sent messages to each of the seven churches to bring repentance and correction to His body of believers. Only two churches came to that spiritual place of true worship: Philadelphia (Revelation 3.10) and Smyrna (Revelation 2:11). They achieved Christ's victorious promises. "Remember therefore from where you have fallen, repent, and do they first work (repentance, prayer, and correction)" (Revelation 2:5).

Chapter 28

The Church in Thyatira: Repent and Meditate on His Word

The time was about AD 1. Thyatira (pronounced "Thai-uh-TAI-ruh") was the location of one of the "seven Christian churches in ancient Greece and a light industry center for makers of such items as cloth, dyes, and copper works." One of the churches was reminded to repent of its soulish and fleshly practices. In Revelation 2:18–26 we read:

> And to the angel of the church in Thyatira write: "The words of the Son of God, who has eyes like a flame of fire, and whose feet are like burnished bronze.

> "I know your works, your love and faith and service and patient endurance, and that your latter works exceed the first. But I have this against you, that you tolerate that woman Jezebel, who calls

herself a prophetess and is teaching and seducing my servants to practice sexual immorality and to eat food sacrificed to idols. I gave her time to repent, but she refuses to repent of her sexual immorality.

"Behold, I will throw her onto a sickbed, and those who commit adultery with her I will throw into great tribulation, unless they repent of her works, and I will strike her children dead. And all the churches will know that I am he who searches mind and heart, and I will give to each of you as your works deserve.

"But to the rest of you in Thyatira, who do not hold this teaching, who have not learned what some call the deep things of Satan, to you I say, I do not lay on you any other burden. Only hold fast what you have until I come. The one who conquers and who keeps my works until the end, to him I will give authority over the nations."

In view of this, the answer is that you must be steadfast in Christ; thus, He will give you the victory! Being steadfast in Christ comes with great victory and ultimate rewards.

Church Observations: Watchman Nee

The soul's attempts to control the spirit of humankind and substitute itself for this spirit of was a significant problem for Watchman Nee (1903–1972), a Christian pastor and teacher. He initiated local Christian churches in China. The soul of humankind and worship must not usurp this authority of the spirit. Every worship service must be conducted in spirit and in truth. As far back as the 1920s, Watchman Nee warned the church that the deadliest deception of the last days was the soulish substitution for the realm of the spirit that would come through technology and music. Satan's tactics include using loud sounds such as drums and microphones. Satan uses a variety of schemes to disguise and deceive the people of God.

Watchman Nee said this:

> We need to guard against anything that initiates emotional response in us, lest we find ourselves depending upon soul power rather than the power of the Spirit of God. The anointing of God can be simulated in the way we modulate our tone of voice or use it as a technological instrument to bring about a certain response. Every time we turn the amplifiers up, or give our voices a little soulish boost and add a little razzmatazz in order to bring an effect, or give an invitation that we know is calculated to play upon the emotional responses of our hearers, then that is false anointing; it is making something like it but it is not the real thing (Holy Spirit).

Chapter 29

Total Salvation is Threefold

The total salvation of a believer is a progressive journey that is "one third human spirit, one third human soul and one third human body." This was a basic belief and teaching of Lester Sumrall (1913–1996), an ordained American Christian pastor and evangelist. Here are a few excerpts from his teachings:

- "You need three steps (1/3 spirit + 1/3 soul + 1/3 body = Son) to receive complete salvation (in spirit, in soul, in body), which completely purifies all three entities before Christ's return (1 Thessalonians 5:23–24). Again, we must be blameless in all three areas of our life."
- "You are not delivered/transferred until your emotions, gratifications, relations, and feelings are refined and gradually emanate to be like Jesus" (Romans 7:23 NASB).

- "Your body (flesh) is not in compliance until you have a Galatians 2:20 experience."
- "Preach and teach the congregation to receive this bread. This Bread, Jesus Christ, came down from heaven. 'Give them fresh Bread by revelation'" (John 6:32–34). [4] Dr Lester Sumrall, *The Human Soul;* The Total Man Series (LeSEA Publishing Co.) South Bend, Indiana. p.11-12.

Demonic Snares: Ignorance or a Lack of Discernment

Countless demonic episodes have been detected. Satan comes into the church with the purpose of wreaking havoc. In the midst of discord and confusion, he attempts to distract many and thereby break up relationships/teams. Thus more confusion arises. Ministers and elders engage in much conflict while there is an open attack within the body of Christ. It is sad to see. "Too often the genuine pastor is removed and replaced by a counterfeit."

1. 2 Timothy 3:1–5
   "This know also, that in the last days perilous times shall come. For men shall be lovers of their own selves, covetous, boasters, proud, blasphemers,

---

[4] Lester Sumrall Evangelistic Association, *The Human Soul*, The Total Man Series (LESEA Publishing, 1984). *Note:* During my period of being stationed in Europe and in Alaska, I was able to see and witness these acts. Some people I could help, and others were not in a position to receive help.

disobedient to parents, unthankful, unholy, without natural affection, trucebreakers, false accusers, incontinent, fierce, despisers of those that are good, traitors, heady, high-minded, lovers of pleasures more than lovers of God; having a form of godliness but denying the power thereof; from such, turn away."

2. Revelation 12:10–11
   "Brethren (believers); sons of God! Our brothers won the victory over him by the blood of the Lamb and by the truth which they proclaimed; and they were willing to give up their lives and die" (GNT).

3. Acts 1:8
   "But ye shall receive power, after that the Holy Ghost is come upon you."

4. John 1:12
   "But as many as received him, to them gave them power to become the sons of God, even to them that believe on his name."

Demonic Behavior

It is very important to reemphasize my point: In all your "getting," get an understanding (by faith receiving God's skillful and godly wisdom) (Proverbs 4:7). This is a critical need and a vital position toachieve, having a full understanding of the will God. The second soul and the third element is the body, on which this book places much emphasis. Only by the spirit of element of the threefold believer is the discernment can we become educated and have a keen understanding. Will the church be able to exercise deliverance to remove these evil spirits and rid the churches of their behavior, especially during times of worship? We will overcome the works of darkness by the Word of God.

It is clearly evident that the goal of demonic spirits is to manifest themselves in order to show contempt for or stop the work of God. The gifts given by the Holy Spirit have been given to the believers to maintain a high standard of holiness. You can read about the various satanic tactics used to hinder or stop the work of God in the book of Revelation.

Soulish Parts (Proverbs 4:7)

Get wisdom and understanding by the Spirit. Solomon reinforces this fact: "In all of thy getting, get an understanding. It is not an option for the believer not to have a revelation concerning the works of darkness that is sent by Satan to defeat the purpose of God." Jesus said to Peter, "I have given you the keys to the kingdom of heaven." Satan works diligently to accomplish his goal of darkness, but the power of God will bring light as promised. However, every believer must be adamant about doing the assigned work of God.

There are at least three dominions or "worlds" in your soulish composition. They involve your (a) *mind*, your thought center, the thinking process arising from the human soul, (b) *emotional life* with your emotions chained together by thoughts and intricately integrated within you—attached together and working in unity, and (c) wrong use of *willpower* in which the soulish human pushes forward and thus engages in wrong decision-making. Satan disguised these tactics so as to kill, steal, and destroy. These acquired attributes are obtained from prolonged exposure to the ways of the world and experiences that blind/stop/limit one from desiring to honor the Father. This type of opposition tends to blind's one desire to live a righteous life. It is a continuing state of blindness unless one cries out to the Father for liberation.

Following are the two foundational scriptures that are the basis of my teaching in order to bring a clear understanding about the body of Christ:

1. "Therefore, without God, a person can become stubborn and very difficult for anybody to get along with. Again, cry out: "Not my will, but Thy will be done" (Luke: 22:42).

2. "I was put to death on the cross with Christ, and I do not live anymore; *it is Christ who lives in me.* I still live in my body, but I live by faith in the Son of God who loves me and gave himself to save me" (Galatians 2:20 NCV).

Born Again. What Next?

As we search the Holy Scriptures, the Father reveals to us that our spirits must be saved, and then the soul and body must be delivered from the woes and hurts of the past (old selfishness full of the past, unredeemed, life). Believe it or not, your soul loves to hold on to the past, which often brings up hurtful memories that are not acceptable for a person living in Christ.

Paul said, "Brothers and sisters, I know that I have not yet reached that goal, but there is one thing I always do. Forgetting the past [negative soulish experiences] and straining toward what is ahead, I keep trying to reach the goal and get the prize for which God called me through Christ to the life above" (Philippians 3:13–14). It is a fact that God made us in His image and likeness. Spirit, soul, and body together is a threefold cord not quickly broken (Ecclesiastes 4:12). Your complete salvation is progressive. You are saved in the spirit, but what I am speaking of are the remaining two entities of your trifold being: the soul and body. This is my prime concern, for you to know that you are in absolute compliance with the Word of God (1 Thessalonians 5:23); if not, then you need spiritual conversion and deliverance for your soul and body.

Great Rewards for the Obedient

If your behaviors are contrary to the Word of God, then your cry and prayer for restoration is your ultimate goal. David said, "Evening and morning and at noon, will

I pray, and cry aloud: and he shall hear my voice. He hath delivered my soul in peace from the battle that was against me: for there were many with me" (Psalm 55:17–18). David also said, "He refreshes and restores my soul (life); He leads me in the paths of righteousness for His name sake" (Psalm 23:3 AB).

Christ, the Truth

In accordance with John 8:36, it is said, "If the Son therefore shall make you free, ye shall be free indeed." Freedom is costly, but every believer needs some form of deliverance. Therefore, your aspiration by revelation is to become His ambassador, and as such you will be pursued, even as the prophet Isaiah said: "The Lord God hath given me the tongue of the learned, that I should know how to speak a word in season to him that is weary: he wakeneth morning by morning, he wakeneth mine ear to hear as the learned. In Isaiah 50:4–5 it is said: "The Lord God hath opened mine ear, and I was not rebellious, neither turned away my back."

Complete Salvation—Sorteria

This goal of complete salvation (spirit, soul, and body) is reachable but not readily accomplished. I am addressing salvation of the soul and body, which need conversion and deliverance, respectively. Even so, the goal is not reachable in such a short duration of time. Remember a great kingdom principle: "In the process of time, God moves in His ways and times." This is my definition of progressive salvation. Your agonizing emotions and feelings that are housed and deep-seated in your soul are what the devil loves for you to look back upon through the eyes of your fallen nature. God knows "your eyes will be opened, and you will be like God, knowing good and evil" (Genesis 3:5), which includes your fallen nature.

Each believer must let the Word of Christ enter inside and also be open to the possibility that the Word of God can renovate our mind-sets, thus allowing us to overcome our problematic and injurious past. "For the Word of God is quick, and powerful, and sharper than any two-edged sword, piercing even to the *dividing asunder of soul and spirit*, and of the joints and marrow, and is a discerner of the thoughts and intents of the heart" [Heb. 4:12]; (emphasis added). It is the Father's expressed purpose to help unto overcome the devastating things that we experienced in the past and become whole again.

The Word of God is powerful to bring a separation of attachment from these issues; separate them; and reorder their alignment. God's Word is alive and is sharper than a double-edged sword; it cuts all the way into us where the soul and the spirit are joined, to the center of our joints and bones. And it judges the thoughts and feelings in our hearts. Nothing in the entire world can be hidden from God; all things are clearly open before Christ. As the Holy Spirit dwells in us, He gives us discerning authority and power to overcome any of Satan's forms of temptations and demonic strategies.

There is long, drawn-out spiritual work assigned by the Father in which the believer must encounter and overcome all manner of opposition. The purpose of this particular opposition is to keep your soul and body free from entanglement with the works of darkness. Our spiritual weapons have power from God that can destroy the enemy strongholds, thus we are able to destroy people's arguments and every proud thing that raises itself against the knowledge of God. Only the Holy Spirit mandates us to capture every thought and make it submit and obey fully. This is the believer's authority and assigned work, to dominate any manner of evil or darkness.

This authority given to the believer must be taught and received in the hearts of the sons and daughters of God. Our thought lives must come into full compliance with the Word of God. The thought life (mind of Christ) is very important because God has given to us the helmet of salvation. Yes, we have been given the helmet of salvation (to restrain our thought lives) as one of our tools for spiritual warfare. We must be careful to obey the Words of our heavenly Father. He told all believers to "put on the whole armor of God, that ye may be able to stand against the wiles of the devil" (Ephesians 6:11). Ephesians 6:17 reads, "And take the helmet of salvation, and the sword of the Spirit, which is the word of God."

God's standard of holiness has been written for our understanding, edification, and compliance. Many believers are deceived in this area in that they do not exercise and fully engage the Word of God. Solomon tells us: "The beginning of wisdom is: Get (skillful and godly) wisdom; it is preeminent. And with all your acquiring, get understanding (actively seek spiritual discernment, mature comprehension, and logical interpretation. And turn away from evil" (Proverbs 3:7).

Chapter 30

Pathway to Salvation

Whole Spiritual Armor

To dress for full protection, provisions and preservation are necessary. "Take the helmet [which is a spiritual symbolic concept—a warring soldier dressed in battle armor] of salvation, and the sword of the Spirit, which is the word of God" (Ephesians 6:17). The helmet of salvation is to protect and support a pure thoughtful life. Without this spiritual protection, our soulish minds will be filled with all kinds of evil, plots, and intentions to implement works of darkness and fall to satanic influences.

We are threefold beings, and the Father's standard for each believer is to come into His expressed order of creation by seeking his or her full compliance with the Word of God. This is my prime reason for saying that salvation is a threefold process, which means full salvation is needed and continues to remain progressive. Again, our souls and bodies are not in full compliance with Christ

Jesus when our soulish minds are ruling. To rule with a soulish mind is an abomination before the Lord. As the soulish mind rules, we will see the manifestation of various kinds of ill-mannered behavior.

Our thought lives or our thinking is not always pure before our Lord because we have violated His creation order. This creation order is firstly the mind of the spirit, secondly the mind of the soul, and lastly the mind of the body. Repentance is required for the spirit mind to fall into divine order. The spirit mind is first, and after it the soul of the mind and the mind of the body come into divine compliance. This is God's recipe for His order of creation coupled with divine favor and great rewards.

Doers of the Word

As you engage in the Word of God as doers of the Word (action in practice), you will walk in victory (Matthew 6:33), regardless of any opposition, which all of us often face. Prophet Isaiah addresses this matter in Isaiah 55:7–8: "Let the wicked forsake his way, and the unrighteous man his thoughts; and let him return unto the Lord, and he will have mercy up him, and to our God, for he will abundantly pardon. For my thoughts are not your thoughts, neither are your ways my ways, saith the Lord." This proves that God is concerned about all believers and wishes for them to adhere to the Word of God.

Mind of Christ

Paul speaks of the importance of having the right mind in spirit, soul, and body. We read in 2 Corinthians 2:16, "Who can know the Lord's thoughts? Who knows enough to teach him? But we understand these things, for we have the mind of Christ" (NLT). In view of this scripture, you must determine whether or not your thought life is in full compliance with the Word of God. It's your responsibility to seek full compliance for your thought life. You have one of two kinds of thinking: pure thoughts or thoughts that offend Jesus Christ.

You must be the judge as to whether your thoughts are established (i.e., whether you are faithful or unbelieving) and in full compliance with 2 Thessalonians 3:3. Remember what Solomon said as you muse on your thought life: "Every heart knows its own bitterness" (Proverbs 4:10). Let us then feel very sure that we can come before God's throne where there is enabling grace. There we can receive mercy and grace to help us when we need it (Hebrews 4:12–13, 16).

Hidden (Stealth) Issues of the Soul and Body

Many negative beliefs, such as one race seeing itself as superior to another, are deeply rooted and ingrained in the human soul and body. Many believers today are plagued with ingrained ancestral and generational problems. It is a fact: We need the power of God's Word to bring forth freedom to deliver our souls and bodies. The Gospel of Mark in chapter 7, verses 21–22, gives us a list to gauge our victory in Christ. Also, the Gospel of Matthew testifies to this same matter in chapter 15, verse 11; evil comes from the heart according to the scriptures. I list two examples as follows:

1. It is true, we have lived in the old ways of tradition. Most of our decisions and actions unadvisedly flow out of the soul's intellect (emotions, feelings, and suggestive ideals), but the Word of God says, "In all thy ways to acknowledge him, so that He will direct your paths."

2. So that we may have a pure heart, Christ wants to deliver us from all past offenses, such as (a) religious habits, (b) familiar spirits that permeate the soul, (c) wrong feeling and negative thoughts, and (d) old memories (Satan is an accuser of your past marriages and sexual partners and of offensive practices embedded in your personality such as racism, discrimination, and hatred).

One major offense is sexual soul ties. (Soul ties are demonic spirits that tie people to an ungodly relationship of the past.) These past sins continue to fight the person's future, other words, many sincere believers cannot grow and become spiritually mature because of the constant false accusations of the powerful enemy. Without true repentance, you can lose the battle of spiritual warfare! Paul says in his letter; "But I discipline my body and bring it into subjection, lest, when I have preached to others, I myself should become disqualified."[I Cor.9:27] Many divorced marriages encounters this type of warfare! "Wherefore come out from among them, and be ye separate, saith the Lord, and touch not the unclean thing; and I will receive you" (2 Corinthians 6:17). "Flee fornication. Every sin that a man doeth is without the body; but he that committeth fornication sinneth against his own body" (1 Corinthians 6:18).

God's Kingdom Principle—Fullness of Joy!

"Thou dost show me the path of life; in thy presence there is fullness of joy [a spiritual position in Christ far above demonic distractions: "Nothing shall offend them!" (Psalm 119:165)]." Furthermore, "At thy right in the right hand there are pleasures for evermore" (Psalm 16:11). "It is not what goes into a man but what comes out that defiles the person" (Mark 7:20–22). Paul says, "Having therefore these promises dearly beloved, let us cleanse ourselves from all filthiness of the flesh and spirit, perfecting holiness in the fear of God" (2 Corinthians 7:1). "By faith, we are called to cast off these things: spiritual darkness and works of evil that hinder the flow and further development of the Holy Spirit in each believer" (Romans 13:11). Only the powerful Holy Spirit overpowers darkness, and it is not easily distracted by the works of Satan. David says in Psalm 119:165 that nothing shall distract him.

The Son's Promise: Freedom and Liberty

Jesus Christ's mandate is to set free His sons and daughters so that they may enjoy the greatness of the freedom He has given them. "If the Son therefore shall make you free, ye shall be free indeed" (John 8:36). Furthermore, God tells us that we must look unto Jesus as the author and finisher of our faith. In the New Century Version of the Bible, we read, "Let us look only to Jesus, the One who began our faith and who make it perfect" (Hebrews 12:2). He paid the price; "He suffered death on the cross." There is a greater price to pay than you think; to be set free from your past is a very extensive and exhausting process, one that is necessary to gain your true discipleship. This true fellowship is freely manifested when the creation of God is in full compliance. The Holy Spirit will flow freely when the believers are in one accord in mind of the spirit, mind of the soul, and mind of the body. "There is much joy in the camp! Behold, how good and how pleasant it is for brethren to dwell together in unity" (Psalm 133:1)! According to Psalm 16:11, when you are on the assigned path, you experience a fullness of joy and pleasures forevermore. Joy, and joy, He freely gives to His sons and daughters!

Are You Born Again from Above?

Initially when you are born again, you cannot fully understand the King and His kingdom. We must understand the fact that full salvation is progressive.

That's a beautiful experience when one comes into the kingdom of God, as such a time as this. Are you born again? Nicodemus, a man of the Pharisees, was confused and he asked, "How can this happen?" Jesus said, "You are an important teacher in Israel, and you don't understand these things?" In other words, being born again is a mystery that only comes from the Father. This mystery is not fully evident; only the Father unveils it for you. "The wind blows where it wants to and you hear the sound of it, but you don't know where the wind comes from or where it is going. It is the same with every person who is born from above by the Holy Spirit. For with the heart man believeth unto righteousness; and with the mouth, confession is made unto salvation" (Romans 10:10). Only the Father from above can save you. I've witnessed preachers telling people they were saved, but there was no witness of their salvation, not then or even later. Finally God is the judge!

Jesus Addressed Nicodemus

Notice that Jesus did not address Nicodemus's attitude, character, or behavior, because the purification process of the soul and body comes into phases of gradual development in the Father's time. In other words, having a complete experience in the kingdom is farther down the road, so to speak. The Father's ways and thoughts are superior, and we are invited to embrace His ways and His higher thoughts. The prophet Isaiah says, "For as the heavens are higher than the earth, so are my ways higher than your ways, and thoughts than your thoughts" (Isaiah 55:9). As we journey in Christ, just as He journeyed, He alone will ensure that we grow in a progressive manner with understanding of the mandates of the kingdom of God. For an example, we are his representatives in the earth, therefore, "Love has been perfected among us in this: that we may have boldness in the day of judgement: because as He is, so are we in this world." [I John 4:17 – [NKJV].

Chapter 31

The Sons' and Daughters' Discipleship

Called to Be His Sons and Daughters

Only the Lord Jesus Christ can bring us forth in His love. John said, "Behold, what manner of love the Father hath bestowed upon us, that we should be called the sons of God." Our Father's resolve is to have a family of sons and daughters. That is His decree. The great invitation comes from the prophet Hosea, who utters the same concern for his sons and daughters: "Come and let us return unto the Lord for he hath torn, and he will heal us; he hath smitten and he will bind us up. After two days will he revive us; in the third day he will raise us up, and we shall live in his sight" (Hosea 6:1–2).

As we journey in the Lord, not only is our calling to go on to Mount Zion, but also we must know (epignosis) Him and be filled with His Spirit of wisdom, knowledge, understanding, counsel, and might, and the fear of the

Lord (Isaiah 11:2). These seven attributes of the Holy Spirit are the nature and character of Christ. Embracing these attributes helps develop us into the image of His Son that He might be the firstborn among many brethren. The first attribute is Christ's presence. Next comes wisdom. Then we are given knowledge as we come to know Him. His counsel entails His directive guidance, which flows out of the Holy Spirit. His might is the strength He gives us, and with the fear of the Lord comes the decision to honor and respect His directives with great reverence.

The hope (Christ Jesus) is to bring many sons and daughters to glory. This is the work of the Holy Spirit—to purify and do more excellent work in every heart. Paul said, "Being confident of this, that he who began a good work in you will carry it on to completion until the day of Christ Jesus" (Philippians 1:6 NIV).

To become one with the Father is His desire for His sons and daughters. "And every man that hath this hope in him purified himself, even as he is pure" (1 John 3:3). This is the progressive method that the Father uses to bring about 100 percent growth in the spirit, soul, and body. God's countless promises are genuine as He has great mercy and grace laid up for His sons and daughters. The apostle Paul says, "Having therefore these promises, dearly beloved, let us cleanse ourselves from all filthiness of the flesh and spirit, perfecting holiness in the fear of God" (2 Corinthians 7:1). This is a divine process of progressive salvation for each of us to behold while experiencing growth and development in Christ.

Chastening

In God's redemptive plan, another kingdom principle is that our Father chastens His sons and daughters, but the disobedient He punishes. No one loves discipline, but God our Father ministers divine discipline to His sons and daughters for His ultimate purpose of spiritual divine alignment. I personally believe that this is the definition of the Father's love and care for His sons and daughters. "My son do not despise the chastening of the Lord, nor be discouraged when you are rebuked by Him" (Hebrews 12:5).

Now that we are saved, we must follow on to know the Lord. The highest level of knowing the Lord is relationship, or epignosis.[5] "Blessed are those who hunger and thirst for righteousness, for they shall be filled" (Matthew 5:6). This is a great promise from our Father, that we will be filled with His Spirit. Then Paul admonishes the sons and daughters to be filled with the Spirit. Once you are emptied of worldliness and are subsequently filled with the Holy Spirit, you have a magnificent spiritual position in Christ.

The prophet Hosea validated the need for change, saying that a human being cannot change himself or herself. Since a human being is a creature of habit, only the Spirit of Christ can help him or her overcome all manner of evil and darkness that's embedded in the soul, keeping the person in lockdown with the past. The dealings of Christ in our lives bring forth the opportunity to be changed/transformed

---

[5] In the biblical sense it means a full understanding of the mystery of God. James Strong, *Strong's Greek and Hebrew Bible*, #1922, s.v. "epignosis."

for good and not evil. It is said in Jeremiah 13:23, "Can a person from Cush change the color of his skin? Can a leopard change his spots? In the same way, Jerusalem, you cannot change and do good, because you are accustomed to doing evil" (NCV). Our assigned destiny is from the Father, to come forth in His image and His likeness.

The Church: The Father's Authority

God said concerning Peter, "Upon this rock, I will build my church and the gates of hell shall not prevail against it. And I will give unto thee the keys of the kingdom of heaven" (Matthew 16:18–19). It is very obvious that some church folks (perhaps unawares) have given over to the works of darkness (untruths, wrong acts, and ill behavior). Satan is a keen master at masquerading as an entity of good and camouflaging himself among God's people. Carnality and deceptions have become dominant activities in many of today's churches, thus opening them up to a natural or carnal mind (not subject to the Holy Spirit). Carnal rules and regulations with hidden agendas do not please the Lord but rather give favor to certain favored ones. These things are contained in the soulish mind and the mind of the body and are manifested in ill behavior. Some believers are highly esteemed with those who respect them being falsely blinded to their hidden motives, whereas others are less esteemed because they have faulty characters and they misbehave. This is blatant activity by those in authority to disrespect the way and standards of Christ.

Spiritually Blind

Unconfessed sins are an eternal bondage. Too often sexual immorality is overlooked from the pulpit to the pews; often Communion is served with some who refuse to repent taking it anyway! This carnal activity and loose living (God said, "Be ye holy; for I am holy") is totally unacceptable because now trust is lacking in the body of Christ. A good example of overlooking the sins of the people (because of one's fear of the people, for varied reasons) is found in 1 Samuel 15:24: "Then Saul said to Samuel, I have sinned; for I have transgressed the command of the Lord and your words, because I feared (fear is resident in the soul) the people and obeyed their voice." When you embrace sin and do not acknowledge your rebellion or stubbornness, you cannot worship the Father in this sinful state. Matthew 15:8–9 says, "These people honor me with their lips, but their heart is far from me." False or pretended worship is not what our Father wants from you. You might go through the acts of worship, but this type of worship is in vain.

The Father's Superiority; Oracles of Christ (1 Peter 4:11)

The Holy Spirit (love of God) is constantly prompting the believer, even the preacher, to repent. This is so clearly evident that God has called the believer to overcome the works of darkness. Again, the enemy attacks the soul and the flesh, but the devil cannot overcome the Holy Spirit.

We have two important examples of an overcoming[6] church in Smyrna and Philadelphia (Revelation 2:8, 3:7). These accounts (referenced earlier) initially are of problematic churches. However, the two (symbolic) women, including the Gerasenes (Mark 5.25) from east of the Sea of Galilee and the Greek Syrophoenician (Mark 6:26), represent a soul- and body-driven church. These examples of churches that are barely striving represent what we are experiencing in the world today. These churches faced constant opposition; however, God did say that the "gates of hell shall not prevail" (Matthew 16:18).

Jesus spoke of God's Word: "Behold, I have given you authority to tread upon serpents and scorpions, and over all the power of the enemy; and nothing shall hurt you" (Luke 10:19). Christ is our ultimate authority, and He has been given authority over the devil (1 Corinthians 15:57). By faith, it is very important to seek and know the way of the kingdom of God. This confirms His message of *expisterio*.[7] Acts 14:22 says: "(Thereby) strengthening the souls of the disciples, encouraging (comforting) them to continue in the faith, and saying that through many tribulations we must enter the kingdom of God."

---

[6] An overcoming church is a church that is victorious over the works of darkness.

[7] Greek word meaning "to strengthen (support) the souls of the disciples."

Chapter 32

Tests Yield Victories

Fiery Trials: Victory in Christ

Jesus said that He left an example and that we should follow in His steps (1 Peter 2:21). Suffering as a Christian is both redemptive and profitable for all believers. It is written in 1 Peter 4:12–14, "My dear friends, do not be surprised at the painful test you are suffering, as though something unusual were happening to you. Rather be glad that you are sharing Christ's sufferings, so that you may be full of joy when his glory is revealed. Happy are you if you are insulted because you are sharing Christ's followers; this means that the glorious spirit, the Spirit of God, is resting on you" (GNT).

Fiery trials are very important—essential, critical—because they enable you to be built up in Him, educated, and established, experiencing divine growth and maturity. A fiery trial may involve being accused of stealing money from the church. This happened to me, but in the end I was given a great reward! The promise word, *established*, is very significant to the sons and daughters of God, "But the Lord is faithful, who shall establish you, keep you from evil?" (2 Thessalonians 3:3). Even when the medical doctor gives you a negative report, your knowing the Lord gives you victory in the midst of the situation. The doctor said you would die in six months, but six years later you are praising God for the victory.

Fiery Trials

Never be ashamed of fiery trials. What is a fiery trial? Paul tells the reader not to be surprised to find himself or herself facing fiery trials. Consider these words of the apostle John: "Because as he is, so are we in this world" (1 John 4:17). Apparently Peter's readers were astonished that they had to suffer as Christians, especially to the extent that they were suffering. The Greek word for "fiery ordeal" is used to speak of the intense fire that burns away impurities in metals. This is an indicator of the internal state of one living above envy, jealousy, and strife, thus placing all distractors under his or her feet. We are spiritually dead, "Many of us were baptized into Christ Jesus were baptized into His death?" Rom. 6:3, and grace continues to abound. The flesh has been subdued, and the Holy Spirit abounds in the believer. The goal of the spirit, soul, and body as understood by Paul is this: "It is no longer I who lives, but it is Christ lives in me" (Galatians 2:20).

Again, Christ is offered up to believers as an example of one who endured sufferings, the Pattern Son: "But … if you endure suffering even when you have done right, God will bless you for it." In 1 Peter 2:21 we read, "It was to this that God called you, for Christ himself suffered for you and left you an example so that you would follow in His steps. He committed no sin." Christ also purifies His sons and daughters according to 1 John 3:3: "And every man that hath this hope in him purifieth himself, even as he is pure." Jesus Christ is our purifier. Each believer is set by grace to overcome (Revelation 12:11)! Putting health issues underfoot by way of faith shows the greatness of God's grace for His servant.

The Spiritual Death: The Believer

The apostle Paul says, "I have been put to death with Christ in the cross. That no flesh should glory in His presence" (1 Corinthians 1:29). Furthermore, he says that true circumcision is parallel to the death of the flesh. Paul defines this as a matter of the heart and not of the flesh. He reveals three aspects: (1) worshipping God in the spirit; (2) rejoicing in Christ; and (3) placing no confidence in any human honor or accomplishment as a means to reach God. It is all about becoming one in Christ Jesus because He and the Father are one. Not only is this a sacred example laid out before us, but also it is a great process we must experience to achieve His standard of salvation concerning our spirit, soul, and body.

Now may God Himself, the God of peace, make you pure, holy, belonging only to Christ. May your whole self—spirit, soul, and body—be protected and without fault (blameless) when our Lord Jesus appears in the last days. You can trust the one who calls you to do that for you (1 Thessalonians 5:23).

Chapter 33

Ultimate Desire in Righteousness

A Prayer for Deliverance

"O, Lord God of my salvation I have cried day and night before thee. …Why hidest thou thy face from me? … Lover and friend, have thou put far from me, and mine acquaintance into darkness" (Psalm 88:1, 14, 18). God loves the body of Christ, and it is His ultimate desire to bless, encourage, and grant unlimited favor to the body of Christ in righteousness. Obedience is much better than sacrifice. God our Father proved His love for us by giving the ultimate sacrifice of His Son Jesus Christ. Jesus paid the price with His body; thereby it is part of the divine order for each of us to pay the price of forgiving one another and loving each other.

It is impossible to love (agape) one another without living out and embracing God's order of creation. I say again, our living must embrace God's mandate that we be saved, first in the mind of the spirit, second in the mind of the soul, and finally in the mind of the body. The believer must seek the Lord to become open to change. It all starts with the inner spirit, the soul, and the body to commit these concerns to Christ. He has promised to answer your cry. If you will only cry out for the Father's help, He will help you (Psalm 30:1–3).

This help will come in the form of the Father's grace. Before you are commissioned and released as king and priest, your heart must be renewed and purified by the Word. All must pay the price of complete salvation, having a spirit mind, a soul mind, and the mind of the body. The compliant prophets Hosea and Malachi speak about the purifications process. It is only by Christ that the believer will experience complete spirit, soul, and body restoration.

Chapter 34

The Father's Call

Sons and Daughters of God

We must come forth in His image and likeness unto the end as Christ's sons and daughters. The prophet Isaiah says it this way: "I will greatly rejoice in the Lord, my soul shall be joyful in my God; for he hath clothed me with the garments of salvation, he hath covered me with the robe of righteousness, as a bride groom decketh himself with ornaments, and as a bride adorneth herself with her jewels. For as the earth bringeth forth her bud, and as the garden causeth the things that are sown in it to spring forth, so, the Lord God will cause righteousness and praise to spring forth before all the nations" (Isaiah 61:10–11).

Redemption (Romans 8.22)

Paul said that creation is waiting for the ultimate manifestation of the sons and daughters of God. The sufferings we have now are not to be compared to the great glory that will be developed and manifested in us, His sons and daughters. Everything God made was changed to become useless, not by its own wish but because God wanted it and because all along there was this hope: "For the creation waits with eager longing for the revealing of the sons of God; for the creation was subjected to futility, not of its own will but by the will of him who subjected it in hope" (Romans 8:19–20 RSV). That is, without Christ we can do nothing. God is holy, and He will not give His power and authority to the unrighteous. Our call is to become one with Christ in spirit, soul, and body; and if we do not, then we are in violation of 1 Thessalonians 5:23.

Special Grace

As servants of God, we are lured by, attracted to, and attacked by the works of darkness once we have reached a certain position. Yet we have the steadfast promises of God for an abundant, fruitful future. We must know and understand that to serve God and to possess His promises causes Satan to rise up against us. John says, "Because as he is, so are we in this world." As a believer you must also know that spiritual warfare has been set in concrete, so to speak, against your life. The Bible says as a witness to you that Satan is an "accuser against the brethren." Satan has risen up to attack your soul (feelings and emotions, and only with a certain amount of success), to discourage you, and even to blot out the very plans that the Father has laid in your heart. God yet remains faithful; you must stay connected to Him in a perpetual relationship.

God visited Joseph with a special calling and gave him a permanent assignment. Sin does not and cannot change His promises; God is superior and all-powerful. Remember, the Father says, "I am God and I change not." Remember also that the Father's plans and purpose for you have not changed. God comes to each of us at an early time in our lives to predestine us to take His chosen path toward our future. God is faithful. He loves you, and you belong to Him. He has designated you to stand in the gap (to perform your given assignment), as do all ambassadors for Christ (2 Corinthians 5:20).

Patriarchs of the Old Testament

At an early age, Joseph, "a proper child," received his assignment as a dreamer, a teen with a kingdom calling and a special journey to represent the Father (see Genesis 37:5–12). At the same time, Satan devised strategies to attempt to cancel this God-given assignment with its mighty promises. The kingdom principle is that the Father says yes to you and tells your accuser the opposite. In other words, God called Moses with an assignment, who then turned and told Pharaoh (Satan) (Exodus 3:4), who hindered this promised and tried to stop it from being realized.

Moses, David, and Paul were loyalists of God. One was known as a man after God's own heart. Romans 7:23–24 tells us that Paul was known temporarily as a wretched man. These three men were murderers; however, God restored these men on used them on earth to represent Him. Forgiveness if you repent is God's great promise to you in order for grace to abound. God's grace is for all who would believe in Him.

Our Father Is Redemptive

In spite of your past actions, the calling upon your life has been reassured and validated by His Word that was previously laid (2 Corinthians 4:7) as a treasure onto your heart at an early age. To further validate Christ's love for you and His ownership of your life, Satan is an accuser and tester of your past life. All that Satan does is to oppose God's promises to His servants. The term "Agape" love and His promise serves as His covenant for your life.

Understanding God's Mercy

By revelation comes divine confidence and trust (Ephesians 3:3). Satan would not attack you if he already possessed you. God's true love is His eternal mercy (compassion) and His unfailing grace as if you had never sinned is evident in His Word. Yet it is true, we have all sinned and come short of His glory, but His grace upholds us far above any past sins. Fight the good fight of faith with this ammunition, the Word of God and His promises to you. Mercy and grace to you. God will surely demolish previous plots against you. Remember how you have been attacked and left with the ingrained spirit of unforgiveness.

Chapter 35

Christ: The King's Final Authority

God has called for an order to creation to operate according to His prescribed plan. I emphasize His order because Satan is the principal deceiver. In many cases, the soul of humankind is operating the church by intellectual knowledge (soulish feelings and emotions), and the Father is not pleased about this. It is the spirit that gives life and never the soul. According to John 6:63, "The flesh profited nothing." Jesus wants to get the body of Christ to go beyond the physical and reach out by faith for the spiritual. Cry out for His enabling grace. Blessings and grace to you as you tackle this issue. This enabling grace will bring you into a spiritual position to please the Father. This is a given: The kingdom of God cannot be shaken. This is the promise referenced in Hebrews 12:25–28.

I hope that you have found your path and that these words have helped you to continue to be strengthened. Hopefully you and others may have a clearer resolve to take up your crosses. I have given you my prayerful understanding, and this message will bless and honor your heart!

> See that you do not refuse Him who speaks. For if they did not escape who refused Him who spoke on earth, much more shall we not escape if we turn away from Him who speaks from heaven, whose voice then shook the earth; but now He has promised, saying, "Yet once more I shake not only the earth, but also heaven." Now this, "yet once more" indicates the removal of those things that are being shaken, as of things that are made, that the things which cannot be shaken may remain. Therefore, since we are receiving a kingdom which cannot be shaken, let us have grace, by which we may serve God acceptably with reverence and godly fear.

Jesus said, "I am the door. ... If anyone enters by me, he will be saved. ... I came that they may have life and have it abundantly" (John 10:10). These are the great and precious promises that the Father has given to His people. Study and meditate on these scriptures and you will discover unfolding riches to bring light into your life along with an understanding of the Father's purpose for your life.

Here is another quotation from the *Amplified Bible* concerning the purity of the soul and body: "For the ruler of the world (Satan) is coming. And he has no claim on me (no power over me and nothing that he can use against me)." Therefore, as the sons and daughters of God come forth in purity of spirit, soul, and body, Satan has no claim on them. Our goal is to come forth in His image and likeness. This is validated by 1 Thessalonians 5:23: "Live blameless and faultless at His appearing." "Ye are witnesses, and God also, how holy and justly and unblameably we behaved ourselves among you that believe" (1 Thessalonians 2:10).

Appendix A

Dr. Sam Soleyn on Salvation

Salvation Is Gradual and Unfolding

A powerful message was preached by Dr. Sam Soleyn on September 10, 2017, at the Thirtieth Apostolic School of Ministry (ASOM) in Johannesburg, South Africa. This sermon is validated by the theological scholarship, doctorate of jurisprudence, commitment to God's Word, and ministry of Dr. Soleyn. He teaches that humanity's salvation is progressive. I contacted Dr. Soleyn concerning his message. He agreed that I may use his quotes to continue validating my spiritual position concerning the subject.

During his sermon he stated;

> The soul and body of every believer needs further ministry in order to come into full compliance with the

Holy Scriptures. There is a divine message for all of us concerning the number three: "On the third day He will raise us up, that we may live in His sight" Hosea 6:2). The God of peace Himself will sanctify you completely; He who calls you is faithful, who also will do it" (1 Thessalonians 5:23–24 KJV). Why? Our Father calls for complete salvation in the spirit, the soul and the body. He promised to help. In 1 Thessalonians 5:23 (KJV), God demands that your spirit, soul and body must be blameless consecrated] at his forthcoming. God's order of creation is progressive salvation—first the spirit, soul and the body—which is destined to be blameless.

Apostle Soleyn, by revelation, noticed that his leaders required further assistance with their inward turmoil (soul). His mature leaders needed a more excellent freedom in their souls. Dr. Soleyn listed vivid examples of how the senior elders of his congregation needed further ministry to be set free. He gave several examples concerning different cases in his church:

It is the Father's desire for his sons to mature in Christ, "But strong meat belongeth to them that are of full age, even those who by reason of use have their senses exercised to discern both good and evil" (Hebrews 5:14 KJV). To hunger and thirst after righteousness is always in the divine order; this is what pleases the Father. Moreover, as the Scripture says, these kinds (forces of evil) come out (soulish entity) by fasting and prayer. It is said in Matthew 17:21 (KJV), "However, this kind does not go out except by prayer and fasting." This is how he rightly discerns the needs of the membership.

God gave him a revelation during his times of fasting and prayer of the spiritual needs in his house in order to free them to elevate them to a higher spiritual level. The Lord began to disclose the varying issues that affect many individual cases, souls that needed to be more accurate in obedience with the spirit. Many of these had great concerns because of the attacks within the soul in which they were kept from breaking through to freedom in Christ with complete deliverance. It is the Father's desire for his sons to mature in Christ.

Issues of the Soul

Dr. Soleyn continued:

> God revealed to him the issues of the soul. How would these emotional pitfalls and strongholds in the soul manifest themselves beyond their ability to reason? Their sufferings, the same emotional issues, were triggered responses from the point of origin. Let's explain with some diagnosis because the Bible gives us a prime example about John the Baptist.
>
> While in the presence of the Holy One, even as a fetus in the womb, the babe leaped. In the book of Luke 1:41 (KJV), it says "… when Elizabeth heard the greetings of Mary that the babe leaped in her womb." Without the ability to see or know any outside activity, this divine act of the Holy Spirit was planted in John. During the second trimester the baby leaped; God created the spirit over the soul; and the soul over the body.
>
> This is God's order of creation. Again, God's creation order is as follows: first the spirit, the soul and then the

body. Furthermore, let's add a little more clarity; the spirit is considered the master; the soul is considered to be the servant; and then the body is the slave. In this case, the spirit of man is superior to the soul of man, and the soul of man is superior to the body of man. When the eyes of the soul are blind, then the soul will easily follow the spirit of man. Both the spirit and soul of man contain the same entities, both have a mind, a will and emotions known as the heart. However, when the mind of the soul is contrary to the mind of the spirit then we have a situation of rebellion, even double mindedness.

It is so; believers do not live under the law of Moses, but instead under the law (Word) of Christ. The living soul in Christ empowers us to love others, which is the fulfillment of the law (Matthew 22:36–40 KJV). Our divine goal is in obeying the Father. "These things I command you, that you love one another" (John 15:17 KJV).

All believers must seek to be more accurate, developing into his image and likeness. The mind of the soul must be subject to, aligned, and compliant with the mind of the spirit which is creation order. Heaven opens when the mind of the spirit has full control over the mind of the soul.

Again, the content of the soul contains the mind, will and emotions. When the soul is non-compliant, out of the emotions flows stress that is manifested when all manner of evil fills and clouds the soul. When the soul mind has dominion over the spirit minds, you're in trouble, because this creates turmoil in your body. Thus, the enemy goal is to bring your life to defeat into the soulish realm, even while in the womb.

Thirty years later, John the Baptist recognized the six-month experience, when he leaped in the womb. Again, when John's initial emotions stirred in pre-natal form, it showed up 30 years later when John the Baptist saw Jesus coming. It is written in Matthew 3:14, "And John tried to prevent Him, saying, I need to be baptized by you, and are you coming to me?" In verse 15, Jesus answered and said to him, "Permit it to be so now, for thus it is fitting for us to fulfill all righteousness. Then he allowed Him."

Satan's Goal: To Kill, Steal, and Destroy (John 10:10)

Now it is Satan's goal to attack the soul via traumatic events. Initially, Satan targets the fetus while in the womb and without the ability to see or experience any activity outside the womb. This classic behavior of the Demonic enemy in this early stage causes a reaction back to the person's soul, thereby causing a further problem in one's life. However, when the soul is in perfect alignment (full compliance) with the spirit, then the body will respond to the spirit because the soul is rightly following the spirit. This is the order of creation.

A "saved soul" is the soul that responds to the mind of the spirit, and the body reflects the choices in the soul (perfect membership). The spirit mind cannot set aside the rule of the soul mind; the soul has to come under the rule of the spirit which often is why you have two emotions going on and your body is confused. The mind of the spirit is telling you something; the mind of the soul is opposing and persistent.

This is a case of double mindedness and you are unstable in your mind. This condition of double mindedness is a ripe recipe for an invitation of such things as diseases. It comes direct from your unsettled nature of the mind of the soul versus the mind of the spirit. When the minds of the spirit and soul are accurate in your life (spirit over soul), then the mind of the soul sees what the mind of the spirit sees; the mind of the spirit looks to the very nature of God. The mind of the spirit was designed to be animated by the Holy Spirit and to open the heavens. So, days of heaven come to earth in your personal circumstances when the mind of the soul is accurately aligned with the mind of the spirit and the heavens open. That's an environment of peace. "He is our peace" (Ephesians 2:14—KJV). At rest! No alarm

Now, by contrast, demonic forces actively torment the mind of the soul while resisting the calming influence of the mind of the spirit under the rule of the Holy Spirit. This is caused when you suffer stress. Again, stress is notably the avenue to which all battles occur; stress freely comes into your environment and you live it out in your body, and you suffer the consequences.

Repentance

Repentance from wrong behavior first leads to take proper actions. When you discover your soul is in trouble, it is because acts that lead to death have now become a priority in your heart; and you should review those things in light of the truth. When you see these things, you will see how the enemy has breached the wall against your efforts to repent. Repentance and remission of sin is in order. When you repent, you re-position the mind of the soul under the rule of the mind of the spirit. When you do that it denies your enemy access to the emotions of your soul.

Again, John the Baptist leaped in the womb of his mother because of the presence of divinity, the unsettling of the soul of his fetus. The soul of John was being alienated in the womb of Mary's body. The fetus of John recognized and instructed his body to jump up and down in his mother's womb. So, when the soul is accurately aligned, his emotions will be translated into activities of joy in the human body. These stirrings in the womb can directly affect your behavior 30 years later like John when he was baptized. All of Judah went out to meet John and thousands were baptized in the Jordan River.

John resisted Jesus and said, "I need you to baptize me." At the same time John, the Baptist saw Jesus coming, and he heard in his spirit that he was the Lamb of God. John learned that Jesus told John that he needed to be baptized. In Matthew 3:14 (KJV) it was said: "And John tried to prevent Him, saying I need to be baptized by you, and are you coming to me?" The Spirit of the Lord told John, 'The one on whom you see, the Holy Spirit, remains on Him. He is it who baptized you with the Holy Spirit and fire when the Holy Spirit descended and remains. Jesus was immediately taken up out of the water and taken into the wilderness to be tempted by the devil." (Matt. 3:13–16)

What basis was John able to recognize Him? Again, the emotions that John experienced in the womb at the age of six months were exactly the same emotions experienced when Jesus stood in front of him (second time in 30 years). So, the things that happen to you in the womb will produce the same emotions thirty years (age of maturity) later. That's why the things you can't remember even so, you behave with proper emotions. You respond emotionally to those things without any ability to recognize why you feel that way. It's a hidden thing. Does that open some things to your head? When you are trying to press through, but it seems like you just can't seem to penetrate this thing and you can't find out what it is; you search back through your memory, but there's nothing there. You can't isolate it.

"Thirty years after he left the womb of his mother, he experienced the identical emotions, when Jesus stood before him. In baptizing thousands in Judea on that basis, why do you come to me to be baptized? This separates Jesus from all of Judea; you must understand the human soul makes decisions not from the basis of reasoning but on the basis of emotions. Then you can understand the importance that your emotions play in the perspective that your soul adopts. In the way God designed the human soul, there must be a delight in the Lord. Psalms 37:4 (KJV) says, "Delight yourself also in the Lord, and He shall give you the desires of your heart." The human soul was meant to give expression to the beauty of God. "Worship the Lord in the beauty of holiness." (True Worship is your prayers, praises, singings, meditations, sacrifices, giving andblessings and praying for others in your church activities are always inspired by the Holy Spirit; never by the soul.) In all of thy ways acknowledge and worship the Lord Jesus. Therefore, your emotions are the most relational aspect in revering our God. It's not your reason that gives expression, to the beauty of God; it's your emotions that gives beauty to God.

Implied Emotional Content: Physical Life and Spiritual Life

Emotional content includes counsel, functions, and morals. Dr. Soleyn continues his sermon, saying,

> You will never find in the Scriptures the term "emotions," but you will find the term heart because the ancients believe when the heart stops, then you are dead. The heart is the key to human relationships. For out of the abundance of the heart, the mouth speaks; out of the heart flows the issues of life. You should love the Lord your God with all your heart, first, then your mind. You may engage your soul mind after your heart is being there. So, God looks upon the heart, while men look on the outward appearance.
>
> So, your enemy understands if he can control the emotions of your heart, then he can control your situations. If the enemy has a choice between your heart and your soul mind, the enemy will always go to control your emotions. Your soul emotions will overthrow the rule of your spirit mind, 'unless' your spirit mind is aligned to the mind of the soul and the Holy Spirit. That is why in the rule of the soul the first priority is not over your emotions but the spirit of your mind, because God gives you your spirit mind to be able to control the behavior. You can't stop feeling the way you feel but what controls how you act is when your spirit mind asserts control over your (soul mind) emotions. So, there is an alignment of mind of the spirit to the mind of the soul heart and body. When the mind of the soul heart is not

in perfect harmony with the mind of the spirit, then your emotions are disclosed as being erratic.

The heart that's within the soul mind is capable of fear. Trauma to your soul mind excites the emotions of fear. The first emotions that Adam put on display when his soul came out of alignment with the spirit was the emotions of fear. Adam said to God, "I heard the sound of your voice in the garden and I was afraid." But until then, when the spirit mind rules the soul mind, he did not know fear.

… God is sovereign over your emotions. So, bring back the mind of your soul under the rule of the mind spirit captures the emotions of fear. We have heard much about God as Father, but we can't access the emotion of the Father toward the son if we think like orphans. When Adam separated himself from his Father, his emotions arose when the mind of the spirit was set aside in favor of the soul. The emotions that arose were fear which causes … you to be crazy. When you are double minded, you will be crazy because you cannot receive anything from the Lord. He doesn't say God doesn't give you anything; it's about receiving; everything about God is true but your ability to receive has been compromised.

The Father's Unconditional Love

Dr. Soleyn talked about unconditional love:

Immediately after Adam's sin, God was still absolutely his Father. But Adam's ability to receive God as his Father was blinded; such action was replaced by the emotions of fear. However, when repentance prevails, the mind of the spirit captures the mind of the soul where emotions lie. To hide from the deliveryman, you have no intent to receive your package. Why? You have already concluded that it is not a gift. So, a double-minded man is one whose soul mind is ruling over the spirit mind and whose emotions in his soul govern his reasons. That is why the cure for that condition is called changing your mind or repositioning your mind. The mind of the soul becomes subsumed under the Lordship of the mind of the spirit. What changes is the double emotions. There's still decision-making out of your (soul) mind but the governing emotions change from fear to life.

Jesus said, "I am come that they might have life, and that they might have life more abundantly" (John 10:10 KJV). And you see God as God is; you see his intentions to give as a gift. The verse says that the soul is the rootstock of unbelief; you don't trust what God has in mind for you even though it is meant to benefit you. You see how this brings everything we have been learning to maturity. Now this root has to do with first and foremost internal rule. We are not going to exercise eternal rule within our sphere if we are eternally frustrated (soulish) in our ability to rule our lives.

Strong Faith: Major Key to Victory

The major key to victory is described by Dr. Soleyn:

The antidote for poison of unbelief is faith. Faith begins by hearing, not by seeing; the mind of the soul works primarily by comparison, the cause and effect by

161

observation, analysis, synthesis and theory are beneficial for stability.

Consider the enemy (Satan) of your emotions. First, refer to Romans 8:7 (KJV). How does the enemy gain access to your emotions? He gains access to your emotions with the intent of stirring up fear through various modes of traumas. His methodology is to set aside the governance of your mind emotions. In the soul, God gave you a mind and God also gave you emotions. The mind is there to govern your emotions so you just won't fly off the handle; you will at least consider the social consequences of the things that follow. These consequences are designed to help you account in sufficient ways to ensure you have maintain the proper emotions. So, if he is able to knock your mind offline and remove it from governing your emotions, then he has strategic access in the guardian of your emotions.

Trauma by definition subjugates and can suspend your logic, reasonable to your emotions. A simple example: If a traumatic event happens in your space you don't say "Let me see how I can analyze the situation." If you are in an accident that is not how you think. You will behave in a rational way. If you are in an accident, you will somehow behave spontaneously. A simple illustration is when your emotions are in charge. If something were to happen to you, your emotions, even in the womb, you will behave the same way in a familiar manner; as this happens, it generally is called a "familiar spirit."

In order to discover the activity of a familiar spirit—that is, to find out whether your emotional response is connected to the facts and circumstances—fasting and prayer are required. Fasting and prayer by the affected person diminishes the importance of the soul. It is an intentional way of bringing back your soul under the rule of the spirit; then God speaks to you and tells you what is causing the problem. This is a major key to your victory.

A note here that needs attention is that special fasting gives the souls a deathly knock down; thus, waiting upon the Lord, the spirit of discernment, (the optimum environment for discernment), "… will reveal to you the issue that's fighting your ability to gain the victory" (1 Corinthians 12:10 & Proverbs 4:7 KJV) in every effort to get an understanding. Discernment is powerful in the environment of fasting. Fasting, usually for 24 hours is more than enough to allow the Holy Spirit to speak to your spirit.

Dr. Soleyn said,

> I finally understood the 50 clients' needs; the Lord wanted to clean up his house and elevate this house's elders to a new level. Therefore, the enemy will not be able to sabotage your growth and purpose in Christ.
>
> Jesus once said to Peter, "… Satan has asked for permission to sift (Luke 22:31–32 KJV) you as wheat, but I have prayed; so, when you turn again; help your brothers …" In another reference Jesus said, "… the enemy is coming (John 14:30 KJV) and he will find nothing in me …" In view of this, where in you will he be able to find something? Will it be in your spirit or soul? Again, Jesus says, "… for the prince of this world cometh, and hath nothing in me." Your spirit is designed to host the presence of God. That's why the evil spirit cannot dwell in the believer's spirit but can dwell in one's soul wherein emotions lie. Evicting the evil spirit out of your emotions is called "saving the soul" (spiritual deliverance).

Paul said in 1 Thessalonians 5:23–25 (KJV), "And I pray God your whole spirit, soul and body be sanctified—be reserve; presented blameless at the coming of the Lord Jesus Christ. He is called faithful, and He will do it."

So, saving of the soul is rescuing you from the control of the enemy so that you will manifest the creativity in the ability as unto the Father, our God. He uniquely put in the soul emotions which will bring your spirit back under control so that your expressions of thought, language, and creativity might shine on earth to the glory of God.

Goal: Obedience

Ways of Men?

"A decision is to be made," explains Dr. Soleyn. He continues,

> In spite of years of erroneous teachings, we have to overcome many religious issues. The soul and body of every believer needs further ministry in order to come into full compliance with the Holy Scriptures. There is a divine message for all of us concerning the third phase of salvation: "On the third day He will raise us up, that we may live in His sight" (Hosea 6:2 KJV). As we live in his sight, we must come to know that Jesus' abundant life has been offered to his sons. "May the God of peace Himself sanctify you completely; He who calls you is faithful, who also will do it" (1 Thessalonians 5:23–24 KJV).

Why? Our Father calls for *complete salvation* (soteria; deliverance, free of bondage) in the spirit, the soul and the body. He promised to help. In 1 Thessalonians 5:23 (KJV), God demands that your spirit, soul and body must be blameless/faultless at his coming. God's order of creation is first the mind of the spirit, the mind of the soul and the mind of the body which is calling forth his sons to be blameless. The Father's desire is to see each son holy unto God. "Love not the world, neither the things that are in the world" (John 2:15–17 KJV).

Fasting to Lift Up the Soul. Freedom, Not Bondage (Isaiah 58:6)

As you cry out to the Father for further development and growth, He is available. To hunger and thirst after righteousness is always in divine order; this is what pleases the Father. Moreover, as the Scripture says, "… these kinds of demonic forces of evil come out by fasting and prayer" (Matthew 17:21 KJV). This is how he rightly discerned the needs of his members in his ministry. God gave him a revelation, during his times of fasting and prayer, of the spiritual needs in his house in order to elevate them to a higher spiritual level. The Lord began to disclose the varying issues that affect the elders of his ministry; souls that needed to be more accurate, gaining full compliance with the Holy Spirit. Many of these had great concerns because of the attacks within the soul area in which they were kept from breaking through to freedom in Christ; complete deliverance.

Appendix B

Progressive Salvation

Appendix C

Get Understanding

Appendix D

God's Creation Order

Glossary

agape love (Greco-Christian). The highest form of love; unconditional love.

epignosis (Greek). Full understanding of the mystery of God.

fellowship. Koinonia; to share in relationships.

gnosis (Greek). Knowledge of the Spirit of God.

huios (Greek). A mature son or daughter who has a spiritual relationship with God.

overcoming church. A church experiencing victory over the works of darkness. It is God who gives us the victory through our Lord Jesus Christ.

sanctification. Progressive process of being made holy or becoming holy.

soma (Greek). Natural body (structure) that has life potentially.

spirit. Pneuma; that part that connects to the Holy Spirit; the creative power of life imbued by God.

soteria (Greek). Deliverance from demonic molestation; freedom from of slavery or bondage.

soul. Psyche; emotions, feelings.

soulish person. One who does not know (spiritually) anything about the Lord Jesus.

teknon (Greek). A nonmature son or daughter developing into maturity.

Printed in the United States
By Bookmasters